BOUTIQUE HOTEL SELECTION

2017

BOUTIQUE HOTEL SELECTION

2017

ALEX BUCHANAN

PRIMO

81 Ridge Road, London N8 9NP

PRIMO is an imprint of Peter Owen Publishers

Primo
An imprint of Peter Owen Publishers
81 Ridge Road
London N8 9NP

A catalogue record for this book is available from the British Library.

Cased ISBN 978-0-9935327-4-0
Paperback ISBN 978-0-9935327-1-9
Epub ISBN 978-0-9935327-5-7
Mobipocket ISBN 978-0-9935327-6-4
PDF ISBN 978-0-9935327-7-1

Designed by Danica Rosso

Printed and bound by Printworks Global Ltd., London/Hong Kong

CONTENTS

INTRODUCING . . .

We have a host of hotel buffs from a wide range of backgrounds to help us find the coolest boutique hotels in the world. Our in-the-know nominations committee members keep their ears to the ground and their pens to paper casting nominee hotels each year. Our unfortunate hotel judges visit each and every nominee, 'working' to understand the guest experience and write up what makes each one unique. Finally, our expert awards panel vote to decide the winners. In total we have over 70 contributing individuals from the nominations committee members, hotel judges and awards panel, all of whom have helped to bring together the select group of hotels you'll find in this book. A very small selection of the team are profiled here.

BRIAN FROELICH
Panellist
The Chairman of JDB Fine Hotels & Resorts, Brian is recognized by *Fortune* magazine as one of travel's most influential executives.

EDWARD GRIFFITHS
Nominations Committee
Currently Chairman of Searcys and Portico Ltd, Edward spent 14 years as Deputy Master of the Royal Household at Buckingham Palace. Knowing – quite literally – what's fit for a king or queen, he makes the perfect addition to our nominations committee.

FRANCISCA KELLETT
Nominations Committee
Travel Editor at the oldest and most drôle glossy lifestyle magazine, *Tatler*, Francisca previously spent six years as Digital Travel Editor at the *Daily Telegraph*.

PAOLO MACCHIAROLI
Panellist
As founder and CEO of My Private Villas – a heavenly collection of the world's most enticing exclusive-use properties – Paolo brings with him 12 years' experience in procuring the finest luxury accommodation.

CHRIS SHEPPARDSON
Panellist
Patron of the Edge Hotel School and architect of the One and All Foundation charity, Chris launched EP Business in Hospitality to help connect businesses and professionals across the world. In addition to publishing three sector magazines and providing business consultancy, the group runs a series of events aimed at encouraging discussion and tackling the keys issues faced by Britain's hospitality industry.

CALLY SQUIRES
Panellist and Hotel Judge
Currently editing *Belgravia* magazine, Cally has written for *The Times*, *Financial Times*, the *Telegraph*, the *Daily Mail* and *GQ* in addition to regular luxury-travel contributions to *Mayfair Times*.

FOREWORD

Despite enjoying access to more of the world than ever before, it can often feel as though all of our choices are inescapably limited. Take a stroll along the winding cobbled streets of Rome or through the genial chaos of Bangkok and the same global brands, products and hotels are present on every corner of every city. Globalization may have enhanced the lives of billions, but it has also made individual experiences that much harder to find.

I started the World Boutique Hotel Awards because I believe that unique destinations – and people – provide the very foundations of our travel adventures. In a faintly suffocating world of uniformity and big-chain hotels, boutique establishments provide the oxygen with which to breathe in new experiences. Independent and family-run, each tells an exceptional story, from the restored 13th-century Tuscan villas and dream-like castle forts in the Indian desert to the secluded beach hideaways and eco-lodges on tropical shores. To identify the very best of these, I formed a team of jet-setting experts and asked them to reveal all: their favourite locations, and why; their unmissable holiday spots; the new, 'undiscovered' places they are dying to visit; and the ones they can't wait to see again.

United in their shared enthusiasm for discovering exciting and unusual destinations, this motley crew of independent industry insiders and luxury-travel specialists then traversed the world to experience each and every property. The result of their travails is this, the *Boutique Hotel Selection*. The definitive guide to our favourite hidden gems in some of the world's most beguiling locations, this book represents our personal collection of the most extraordinary boutique destinations on earth. Ultimately, getting to know the heart and soul of our boutique hotels is at the core of what we do.

Edward Gabbai
Founder and Director, World Boutique Hotel Awards

An *unsurpassed collection*
of the finest and most unique properties

Hotels are selected based on their location, reputation, distinctive facilities, value and, most importantly, their caring, personal approach to their guests. Selling in the USA exclusively through travel agents, JDB's staff of well-travelled professionals provide superb personal service.

FINE HOTELS JDB & RESORTS

THE *hush* COLLECTION

jdbhotels.com | thehushcollection.com

AFRICA

26 SUNSET VILLA

Cape Town, South Africa

High above Llandudno Bay this beautiful exclusive-use clifftop property encourages guests to enjoy life in pure sequestered luxury:

6 SUITES AVAILABLE EXCLUSIVELY BEACH COMPLIMENTARY CANAPÉS AND SUNDOWNERS DRINKS INCLUDED HOME OFFICE FACILITIES OVERSIZED BATHS AND RAIN SHOWERS PRIVATE CHEF AND BUTLER SERVICE SOLAR-HEATED POOL AND STEAM ROOM

26 SUNSET VILLA, LLANDUDNO, CAPE TOWN, 7806, SOUTH AFRICA
+44 208 672 7040 | LLANDUDNO@26SUNSETVILLA.COM | 26SUNSETVILLA.COM

BOUTIQUE HOTEL SELECTION 12 AFRICA

After a few days at 26 Sunset Villa it becomes very, very hard to contemplate ever returning to normality.

For travellers, awakening to the sound of breaking waves on a beach is akin to hearing, quite literally, the sound of one's dreams. Ignoring for a moment its relative ineffectiveness as an alarm call, the sound of the ocean is nevertheless a potent reminder that life back home has been left behind. At 26 Sunset Villa, the reverie becomes a reality.

This African gem sits alone on the hillside between the effortlessly trendy Camp's Bay and the peaceful town of Hout Bay. Warmly decorated with a blend of natural stone and wood tones, the air-conditioned interior is fitted with floor-to-ceiling windows, private balconies, underfloor heating and retractable glass doors. Leading directly onto a private deck, these provide access to the villa's 180-degree views of mountains, oceans and the fabled South African sunsets.

Inside, the six identical suites are served by a butler, private chef and villa manager, all of whom excel at the skill of being immediately present when required and virtually invisible when not. Breakfast may be as swift as a simple Nespresso or as elaborate as a champagne four-course feast, with lunches and canapé-led dinners also a speciality. Unsurprisingly, after a few days of this it becomes very, very hard to contemplate ever returning to normality.

Similarly, there are more than a few distractions competing for one's attention on the outside, too. In addition to the private solar-heated pool and steam room, the deserted beach below makes it hard to resist the seduction of lava-hot sand on tired toes. A word to the wise, however: those who value the use of their feet should resist the temptation to streak impetuously into the sea. Flowing straight from Antarctica, the crystalline water is as chilling and deceptive as it is alluring. That said, there are few more entertaining activities than observing, from the comfort of the villa balcony, uninitiated first-timers running blithely into the breaking waves. The spectacle of undisguised horror as the magnitude of their naivety becomes apparent is oddly addictive and frequently hilarious. Sundowners and *schadenfreude* never tasted so good.

Fortunately, the sights of breaching whales or pods of dolphins approaching the shore inevitably lend a conciliatory air and to witness either in person is to capture the essence of this tortuously pretty corner of Cape Town. With that in mind, if the Mother City appears on a travel itinerary in the coming months, be sure to book a few days at 26 Sunset Villa. Radiating indulgence, friendliness and typical South African hospitality in this beguiling residential suburb, there are few places on Earth that can match it for all-round irresistibility. BHS

PONDORO SAFARI LODGE

Limpopo, South Africa

Situated on the banks of the Olifants River, this award-winning luxury game lodge enhances a true African safari like a good Shiraz complements a steak.

8 ROOMS   AIR CONDITIONING   BAR   GYM   POOL   RESTAURANT   SPA   WINE CELLAR

PONDORO SAFARI LODGE, BALULE NATURE RESERVE, GREATER KRUGER NATIONAL PARK, HOEDSPRUIT, 1380, SOUTH AFRICA
+ 27 317 645 049 | RESERVATIONS@PONDORO.CO.ZA | WWW.PONDORO.CO.ZA

BOUTIQUE HOTEL SELECTION   14   AFRICA

Located within the 50,000-hectare Balule Private Nature Reserve, which itself forms part of the Greater Kruger National Park, Pondoro represents the best of both worlds. For visitors seeking a less touristy safari experience but with the highest possible chance of seeing the 'Big Five' in action, smaller private game reserves such as this are often the way to go.

Established in 1997 by Robbie and Lize Prehn, Pondoro has grown into one of the country's most respected five-star lodges. With five luxury suites and three chalets it is sufficiently engaging for guests who like to mingle, yet quiet and refined enough to provide privacy and exclusivity for those who would rather not.

Equipped with private patio, lounge area and outdoor Jacuzzi, each suite is air-conditioned and furnished with typical African style. Nearby, the equally well-cooled ensuite chalets benefit from freestanding baths, wooden decking and attendant views – occasionally of passing wildlife – over the Olifants River.

Naturally, like the best boutique establishments, Pondoro enjoys mixing it up a bit when the mood takes them, hence the construction some years ago of a large treehouse secreted deep in the bush. Designed for visitors who prefer a more feral side to their accommodation, this unique structure overlooks a spot-lit watering hole in a prime position within the park. Safely dropped off after dinner and effectively left to one's own devices within the treehouse itself, guests may either stay up or snuggle up

ROBBIE AND LIZE PREHN

until collection during the game drive the following morning.

And what a drive it is likely to be. The park's unique position within the Greater Kruger area affords everyone the opportunity to witness animals in their natural habitat, without themselves being herded around by the larger tour operators. As well as the must-see lion, buffalo, leopard, rhino and African elephant, the reserve offers a healthy chance of glimpsing cheetahs and the even the ultra-rare black rhino.

With owner Robbie as ranger, aided by a local tracker, following up a potential sighting can prove as frenetic and exciting as the eventual result. Excursions into the bush are further helped by thoughtful Pondoro touches like the provision of heated beanbags on truck seats during chilly mornings. Likewise, there are nature walks on offer during the day to supplement the dawn-and-dusk activities.

Afterwards, when exhaustion from an early start and full day's excitement have taken their toll, the lodge's Serenity Spa will coax even the weariest bodies back into balance. Featuring a glass-covered steam room, outdoor spa bath and full massage facilities, the spa also offers an extensive range of traditional South African treatments and remedies

Perhaps unsurprisingly, the dining experience at Pondoro is as engaging and romantic as are the game drives and accommodation. A fusion of traditional African and modern European cuisine, the menus feature local specialities including buffalo, ostrich and springbok steaks, accompanied by an extensive cellar and whisky collection. As a two-time recipient of the Diners Club Platinum Award for their wine list, the Lodge is well-known for serving some of the finest food and drink in the area.

With that in mind, when the opportunity next presents itself to experience a 'Big Five' safari in the Kruger National Park, make sure it includes a few nights at Pondoro Game Lodge. Its warm welcome, luxury accommodation and relaxing atmosphere all contribute to a truly authentic game-viewing experience under African skies. **BHS**

Arriving at Balule Nature Reserve in 1997 armed with nothing more than a dream and a truckload of faith, Robbie channelled his love of wildlife into designing and building the lodge. His insistence from the outset on prioritizing the welfare of the animals soon began to pay off, as the reserve became renowned for great game viewing. Later, when his future wife joined him, she brought with her a natural flair for cuisine and used her artistic background to influence the detail and décor within the lodge. Two decades on, the staff at Pondoro represent the heart of this exceptional retreat, and every member of the team is considered part of the same big family.

ROYAL MANSOUR

Marrakesh, Morocco

Set within the walls of the old city and bearing the hallmark of His Majesty Mohamed VI, King of Morocco, this outstanding hotel is a masterpiece of style, character and craftsmanship.

53 RIADS/SUITES 3 RESTAURANTS 24-HOUR BUTLER SERVICE ART GALLERY BAR FITNESS CENTRE
INDOOR/OUTDOOR SWIMMING POOLS LIBRARY MICHELIN-STARRED CHEF SPA

ROYAL MANSOUR, RUE ABOU ABBAS EL SEBTI, MARRAKESH, 40000, MOROCCO
+ 212 5 29 80 80 80 | INFO@ROYALMANSOUR.MA | WWW.ROYALMANSOUR.COM

BOUTIQUE
HOTEL   18   AFRICA
SELECTION

Having enjoyed a period of consistent growth, helped in part by a rapid increase in the number of riads available for rent, Marrakesh's tourism economy has over the last few years remained relatively buoyant.

Replicating a traditional medina, complete with gardens, courtyards, mosaics, fountains and winding paths, the Royal Mansour is arguably one of the city's greatest assets. With a courtyard-fountain, reception room and up to four bedrooms apiece, these three-storey traditional Moroccan dwellings have proved exceptionally popular with families, newlyweds and groups alike. Well-known for their panoramic roof terraces and rich furnishings, the riads of Marrakesh are among the city's most compelling draws.

Lavishly equipped with cedarwood doors, plunge pools, sunbeds, mosaic floors and exquisite antiques, these terracotta-coloured mini-palaces are served by genial hotel staff via a network of ingenious underground tunnels. If it all sounds very James Bond, that's because it is.

The hotel's trio of restaurants – one of which is widely believed to be the best of its kind in Africa – are overseen by Three-Michelin-Starred chef Yannick Alléno. Meanwhile, the traditional hammam, the swimming pool and the hotel's extensive gardens have all been designed to cosset and restore guests after their exploratory efforts around the city. Creating personalized programmes in addition to a comprehensive range of traditional classes and treatments, the spa here is as close as it comes to sublimity. From yoga, Pilates,

massage and steam therapies, to nutrition, exercise, wellbeing and stress management, everything is designed to help achieve a specific health-orientated goal.

And with a new extension comprising a 1.5-hectare garden, a 600-square-metre pool adorned with pavilions and a fourth restaurant supervised by Yannick himself, the Royal Mansour represents the ultimate Moroccan escape.

Originally commissioned and owned by the King of Morocco, Mohamed VI, the palace plays host to an international clientele eager to experience the Moroccan lifestyle. When the rooftop views, sprawling gardens and nearby Atlas Mountains are taken into consideration, it quickly becomes clear that there is simply no reason to stay anywhere else. BHS

EL FENN
Marrakesh, Morocco

Replete with historic architecture and Moroccan grandeur, this über-chic hotel sits on the edge of the famous Medina, within walking distance of the city's major attractions.

With its open-wood fireplaces, hand-carved cedar ceilings, leather-lined walls and artisan-crafted plasterwork, El Fenn is a lavishly detailed, gloriously extravagant establishment that is well worth visiting for as long as budgets allow.

Tucked away down a side street and hidden among tree-filled courtyards, the thick walls of this palatial establishment hide a labyrinth of rooms, suites and open spaces. Each room or suite is styled individually, and many are equipped with high ceilings, monsoon showers and deep bathtubs. For an extra layer of luxury and exclusivity, there are several two-, three-, four- and five-bed private 'houses' also available just a minute or two from the main hotel. Epitomizing the El Fenn experience, these exclusive riads represent the ultimate accommodation and come complete with kitchen, private dining area and roof terrace, and all bar one have a plunge pool. In fact, as one of the few properties in Marrakesh equipped with a swimming pool – two, as it happens – the hotel earns its place among the most sought-after establishments in the city. Lined in Carrara marble, the presence of the pools is as welcome as it is humane, in a country where peak temperatures regularly nudge 40 degrees Celsius. Likewise, an hour or two relaxing on a daybed in the rooftop Berber tent or submerging oneself in the plunge pool may also help alleviate the effects of the relentless heat, as will a wander in the cooler courtyard gardens. There is a welcome, thoroughly refreshing absence of televisions in the rooms at El Fenn. Instead, guests are invited to abandon their digital shackles and fully recharge *themselves* for a change.

Naturally, sustenance and refreshment take centre stage at El Fenn, and the hotel's cocktail bar and restaurant provide deep sofas and vintage armchairs in which to relax. Surrounded by potted palms, arresting artworks and accompanied by a colourful menu showcasing the most alluring Moroccan and European dishes,

---

28 ROOMS   LIBRARY   ROOF RESTAURANT/TERRACE   SPA AND HAMMAM   SWIMMING POOL   TURTLES IN THE LOBBY

EL FENN, DERB MOULLAY ABDULLAH BEN HEZZIAN, BAB EL KSOUR, MEDINA, MARRAKESH, MOROCCO
+212 524 44 1210 | CONTACT@EL-FENN.COM | WWW.EL-FENN.COM

BOUTIQUE HOTEL SELECTION   21   AFRICA

© David Loftus, El Fenn

© Laila Alaoui, El Fenn

guests may enjoy meals either in the restaurant or the comfort of their own rooms and private houses. On warmer evenings, dinner is served al fresco on the 650-square-metre roof terrace, with the city lights blinking away in the background. In among them, in the shadow of the mighty Atlas Mountains, the decorative arches and 80-metre minaret of Marrakesh's beautiful mosque, the Koutoubia, stands out above the city's skyline. Dating from the 12th century and stunningly illuminated at night, it reliably attracts large numbers of worshippers, visitors and inquisitive tourists who are naturally drawn to both its spirituality and its setting.

Meanwhile, the hotel's candlelit spa offers a range of traditional beauty rituals, including massages, black soap scrubs and Ghassoul clay body-masks applied in the authentic hammam. Using specialist Moroccan skin products created by Les Sens de Marrakesh, the in-house therapists administer a series of indigenous treatments using Argan-based massage oil. Found only in Morocco, this rarity is rich in Vitamin E and linoleic acid and is known for its anti-inflammatory and healing properties. Alongside these treatments, personal training sessions, yoga and pilates are available on the roof terrace, with the city's hectic, genial atmosphere providing a stark but fascinating contrast in the background. For the more active or adventurous visitor, sightseeing and exercise may be combined through personalized jogging tours and cycling trips* around the medina. There are plentiful golf courses from which to choose, and the local hills and mountains provide a challenging day's hiking.

With its open-wood fireplaces, hand-carved cedar ceilings, leather-lined walls and artisan-crafted plasterwork, El Fenn is, in short, a lavishly detailed, gloriously extravagant establishment that is well worth visiting for as long as budgets allow. **BHS**

VANESSA BRANSON AND HOWELL JAMES

Searching 15 years ago for a holiday home in Marrakesh, Vanessa and Howell came across a dilapidated courtyard in a former private house. Following an exhaustive two-year renovation, Vanessa eventually opened El Fenn as a six-bedroom hotel. Since then, having purchased and converted several neighbouring riads, the couple have added three swimming pools, a bar, a spa, a restaurant, a library and a total of 22 further bedrooms. Thanks to the meticulous renovation and interior design by El Fenn's General Manager, Willem Smit, the project has been transformed into a luxury Moroccan retreat in a most captivating African environment.

* For groups of up to six people.

RIVER BEND LODGE

Eastern Cape, South Africa

Set within a 14,000-hectare private concession – which itself forms part of the malaria-free Addo Elephant National Park – this exclusive lodge presents the perfect balance between the elegance of colonial country life and the wilds of the Eastern Cape bush.

8 SUITES · EXCLUSIVE-USE VILLA · GAME DRIVES · HONEYMOON SUITE

RIVER BEND LODGE, ZUURBERG ROAD, ADDO ELEPHANT NATIONAL PARK, ADDO, 6105, EASTERN CAPE, SOUTH AFRICA
+27 42 233 8000 | RESERVATIONS@RIVERBENDLODGE.CO.ZA | WWW.RIVERBENDLODGE.CO.ZA

BOUTIQUE
HOTEL   24   AFRICA
SELECTION

© David Loftus, El Fenn

© Laila Alaoui, El Fenn

VANESSA BRANSON AND HOWELL JAMES

Searching 15 years ago for a holiday home in Marrakesh, Vanessa and Howell came across a dilapidated courtyard in a former private house. Following an exhaustive two-year renovation, Vanessa eventually opened El Fenn as a six-bedroom hotel. Since then, having purchased and converted several neighbouring riads, the couple have added three swimming pools, a bar, a spa, a restaurant, a library and a total of 22 further bedrooms. Thanks to the meticulous renovation and interior design by El Fenn's General Manager, Willem Smit, the project has been transformed into a luxury Moroccan retreat in a most captivating African environment.

guests may enjoy meals either in the restaurant or the comfort of their own rooms and private houses. On warmer evenings, dinner is served al fresco on the 650-square-metre roof terrace, with the city lights blinking away in the background. In among them, in the shadow of the mighty Atlas Mountains, the decorative arches and 80-metre minaret of Marrakesh's beautiful mosque, the Koutoubia, stands out above the city's skyline. Dating from the 12th century and stunningly illuminated at night, it reliably attracts large numbers of worshippers, visitors and inquisitive tourists who are naturally drawn to both its spirituality and its setting.

Meanwhile, the hotel's candlelit spa offers a range of traditional beauty rituals, including massages, black soap scrubs and Ghassoul clay body-masks applied in the authentic hammam. Using specialist Moroccan skin products created by Les Sens de Marrakesh, the in-house therapists administer a series of indigenous treatments using Argan-based massage oil. Found only in Morocco, this rarity is rich in Vitamin E and linoleic acid and is known for its anti-inflammatory and healing properties. Alongside these treatments, personal training sessions, yoga and pilates are available on the roof terrace, with the city's hectic, genial atmosphere providing a stark but fascinating contrast in the background. For the more active or adventurous visitor, sightseeing and exercise may be combined through personalized jogging tours and cycling trips* around the medina. There are plentiful golf courses from which to choose, and the local hills and mountains provide a challenging day's hiking.

With its open-wood fireplaces, hand-carved cedar ceilings, leather-lined walls and artisan-crafted plasterwork, El Fenn is, in short, a lavishly detailed, gloriously extravagant establishment that is well worth visiting for as long as budgets allow. **BHS**

* For groups of up to six people.

RIVER BEND LODGE

Eastern Cape, South Africa

Set within a 14,000-hectare private concession – which itself forms part of the malaria-free Addo Elephant National Park – this exclusive lodge presents the perfect balance between the elegance of colonial country life and the wilds of the Eastern Cape bush.

8 SUITES   EXCLUSIVE-USE VILLA   GAME DRIVES   HONEYMOON SUITE

RIVER BEND LODGE, ZUURBERG ROAD, ADDO ELEPHANT NATIONAL PARK, ADDO, 6105, EASTERN CAPE, SOUTH AFRICA
+27 42 233 8000 | RESERVATIONS@RIVERBENDLODGE.CO.ZA | WWW.RIVERBENDLODGE.CO.ZA

As a true family destination where children are welcomed and special care is taken to ensure that all ages are entertained, River Bend Lodge presents a unique wilderness experience.

From its location on a private concession within the famous Addo Elephant National Park, River Bend Lodge enjoys a reputation as a world-class culinary and photographic destination. Home to an abundance of wildlife, the Lodge comprises eight luxury standalone suites, one being the honeymoon suite, linked by a meandering path. The colonial-style interiors are fully equipped with modern comforts and amenities, and each suite has its own private patio. There is a central lounge, dining-room, day room and bar where one can enjoy delicious meals and interesting wines.

The bush walks and game drives uncover a catalogue of nature's must-see wildlife. Accommodating over 300 species of bird and the so-called 'Big Five' – the elephant, rhino, leopard, lion and buffalo – everything is here, and the difference in experience with the larger reserves is stark. Whereas the big commercial operations commonly view visitors merely as part of the numbers game, at River Bend Lodge the staff enjoy becoming acquainted by name. And as one of the few such game reserves to employ a permanent in-house professional photographer, the estate will assist with one of the most sought-after skills on an African safari: capturing the seminal moment on camera. After all, there is little point in expending considerable amounts of time, effort and money on the trip of a lifetime, only to return with a few hastily taken snaps of the back end of a rhino.

Naturally, the cuisine here far exceeds its brief of keeping energy levels pumped for long enough to last through the endless, hot summer days and sociable evenings. Dishes prepared in the style of traditional European and Pan-African cuisine and accompanied by hand-picked wines from around the country are served in the Silver Thorns Restaurant, which is as much a showcase for the chefs as the terrain outside is a grandstand for the wild beasts

And as a true family destination where children are welcomed and special care is taken to ensure that all ages are entertained, River Bend Lodge presents a unique wilderness experience. Replete with home comforts, superb hospitality and famous for its life-changing elephant encounters, this special destination enables guests to enter truly into the spirit of South African life. BHS

RHULANI SAFARI LODGE

Madikwe, South Africa

An authentic, extravagant African safari lodge offering peace, luxury and astonishing game drives in the rolling grasslands of Madikwe Game Reserve.

7 LUXURY CHALETS   BARS   POOL   RESTAURANT

RHULANI SAFARI LODGE, MADIKWE NATURE RESERVE, MADIKWE, 2874, SOUTH AFRICA
+27 14 553 3981 | RESERVATIONS@RHULANI.COM | WWW.RHULANI.COM

BOUTIQUE
HOTEL   26   AFRICA
SELECTION

At 75,000 hectares and with a strong reputation for delivering the so-called 'Big Five' and 'Magnificent Seven' in action, Madikwe is among the largest game reserves in South Africa. Established over 25 years ago in the country's North-West Province, it is home to several endangered species including the black rhino and the African wild dog, among many others.

Positioned on the edge of the bush overlooking the reserve itself and each blessed with outdoor large deck and plunge pool, Rhulani's seven luxury detached chalets bring the beauty of the wild to discerning guests. The spacious, minimalist interiors may be further extended by adding two stretcher beds for children, while the single luxury family suite comprises dual bedrooms, each big enough for two adults. Family-flexible, the sofa in the communal lounge here may also be converted into a couple of further berths for additional guests. Equipped with four-poster bed, air conditioning, outdoor shower and enormous bathtub, all the lodges at Rhulani give the distinct impression of being sophisticated urban hotel rooms, and yet the view from the windows reliably suggests otherwise.

This being Africa, dining al fresco is a part of everyday life and a three-course meal under the stars, accompanied by a selection of world-class local wines, is an opportunity that should not be passed up; listening to the sounds of a nature reserve that appears as lively at night as it is during the day proves an eye-widening experience, and not merely because of the quality of the traditional-style cuisine; the scene itself changes night on night as the dinner location moves around the property.

Having cosied up for an evening by the fire back at the lodge, an experienced ranger signals the reveille for Rhulani's early-morning game drives. Providing a legendary safari experience, these friendly, charismatic guides know exactly where to find the all-important elephant, buffalo, lion, rhino and the super-elusive leopard in addition to giraffe and zebra. Depending on a number of factors, of which pure chance is inevitably one, the drive may also yield sightings of cheetah, African wild dog, spotted hyena and several of Madikwe's 350 species of bird. And if the gods really are smiling down on the day, the sight of lions or leopards feasting after a morning kill is simply one of life's most sobering-yet-rewarding moments. Put bluntly, it's what you came for.

In between the morning and evening game drives, a spot of R&R is highly recommended. Fortunately, the lodge's own swimming pool overlooks a popular watering hole, providing a tidy metaphor as cocktails are served on the sun-loungers. If time permits, Rhulani's extensive spa menu allows a few hours' respite from the relentless sights, sounds and smells of this beautiful retreat, with the experienced therapists dispensing all manner of exotic treatments.

All of which neatly sums up life at Rhulani: Swiss-owned and staffed with a local team, the lodge fuses the highest standards in European and African hospitality with quick, easy access to the most spectacular game drives. Super-exclusive and with no teeming crowds of tourists to ruin the mood, Rhulani is an unforgettable way to enjoy a luxurious but genuine South African safari experience. BHS

GRAND DÉDALE
COUNTRY HOUSE

Western Cape, South Africa

This exclusive-use manor house presents a tempting proposition for outdoor pursuits, vinous indulgence and poolside recuperation in the captivating Cape Winelands.

7 ROOMS AND COTTAGE · SALTWATER POOL · AL FRESCO DINING · GOURMET BARBEQUE FACILITIES

HONESTY BAR · MULTI-LINGUAL SENIOR STAFF · RESTAURANT · SPA ROOM AND TREATMENTS

GRAND DÉDALE COUNTRY HOUSE, RUSTENBERG ROAD, THE BOVLEI, WELLINGTON, 7654, SOUTH AFRICA
+27 21 873 4089 | INFO@GRANDDEDALE.COM | WWW.GRANDDEDALE.COM

BOUTIQUE
HOTEL   28   AFRICA
SELECTION

Of all the countries in the Southern hemisphere, none is as beguiling, contradictory and helplessly addictive as South Africa. The striking scenery and boundless opportunities for adventure make it one of the most popular travel destinations on the continent, and the Western Cape plays a notable role in its overall allure. With a compelling combination of temperate climate, arresting vistas, friendly people and liberated lifestyle, this southern province is, for many, the most irresistible location in the world. Largely responsible for much of this popularity and goodwill, the vineyards and wine routes of Paarl, Franschhoek and Stellenbosch draw the discerning traveller like a powerful magnet, and when Grand Dédale opened as a luxury hotel in 2009 it was in direct response to this demand.

Offering arguably the most captivating, untamed setting on its side of the equator, the recently restored colonial manor house lies at the end of a long valley below the historic Bainskloof Pass. Dating back to the early 1700s and surrounded by hundreds of hectares of impossibly pretty countryside, the estate has gained a justifiable reputation as a world-class winery. Once the private residence of the former owner of the nearby Doolhof wine estate, the house comprises a total of six bespoke bedrooms and suite. Ranging in size from 32 to 63 square metres, each enjoys views of the gardens or mountains, while the adjacent restored thatched cottage adds over 100 square metres of additional space and privacy. The former wine store is now a delightful cottage for

additional guests. This may be booked as a chapel for wedding ceremonies, or as a function venue.

Facing eternally distracting views of the Groenberg, Limietberge and Hawekwa mountains, guests are presented with a stark choice: laze around beside the 15-metre swimming pool all day, perhaps enjoying a visit from the local professional spa therapist; or venture out to participate in several of the innumerable activities in the surrounding area. This being South Africa, the potential for constant diversions and entertainment is all but limitless, and working out how to fit everything in to the holiday schedule can prove something of a challenge in itself. Walking, quad-biking and cycling may be a given, but so is riding, river-rafting, golf and clay-pigeon shooting. Then is the trout fishing, hot-air ballooning, picnic hikes and the world-class wine-tasting trips. And when the active part of the day is complete, the full selection

of Doolhof's award-winning labels are available for sampling in the estate's tasting room. Private tours of the cellar may also be organized and are a fitting prelude to the four-course table d'hôte evening meal. Devised and prepared daily by the estate's resident chef, the menu features a showcase of the highest quality South African ingredients utilizing the freshest meat, game, fish and vegetables from the local area. Served either in the hotel's private dining-rooms or al fresco on the grand veranda overlooking the mountains, it highlights Grand Dédale's status as a shrine to good food and wine. And that, essentially, sums up the philosophy of this extraordinary retreat; to combine exceptional hospitality with first-class fare and a companion or group of friends is one thing, but when these are blended with glorious landscapes, vivid sunsets and luxurious accommodation, it becomes an altogether more irresistible proposition. BHS

GORMLEY & GAMBLE

SAVILE ROW FOR WOMEN

Made-to-measure jackets, coats, shirts, dresses and trousers

By appointment only

www.gormleyandgamble.com

GORMLEY & GAMBLE | 13 SAVILE ROW | W1S 3NE

AMERICAS & CARIBBEAN

BHS

ENTRE CIELOS

Luján de Cuyo, Argentina

Secreted away in the foothills of Argentina's finest wine region, this utterly distinctive hotel and hammam spa presents pure Latin American luxury for wine aficionados.

16 ROOMS OUTDOOR HEALTH CIRCUIT **POOL BAR** RESTAURANT **SPA** VINEYARD

ENTRE CIELOS, GUARDIA VIEJA 1998, VISTALBA, 5509 LUJÁN DE CUYO, ARGENTINA
+ 54 261 524 48 90 | HOTEL@ENTRECIELOS.COM | WWW.ENTRECIELOS.COM

As the ultimate destination for rest and outstanding vinous indulgence, Entre Cielos fuses modern comforts, ancient rituals and award-winning wines to create a world-class sanctuary for body, soul, spirit and palate.

Sitting on eight hectares in one of the largest wine-producing regions in Latin America, Entre Cielos is located deep in the vineyard-filled Mendoza countryside.

The dream of three Swiss friends who purchased and converted the land in 2009, the unique development includes 16 suites, each individually styled on different wines.

From the flagship Grand Cru master suite with its private terrace, rainforest shower and outdoor Jacuzzi, to the stilted Rosa Blanca's balcony-bathtub and vineyard views, the accommodation is as exclusive and unfettered as it is quirky and quiet.

And as the first traditional six-circuit hammam spa in South America, Entre Cielos stands alone, both in foresight and facilities. Originating in the Orient over a thousand years ago, the hammam tradition became part of the bathing ritual in Arabic, Greek, Roman and Turkish cultures. As the participant progresses through the various steam rooms and bathing pools, the combination of heat, water and massage techniques helps rid the body of accumulated toxins. Meanwhile, Entre Cielos's own bespoke range of vinotherapy treatments, including grapeseed exfoliation and grape-extract wine baths, complement and enhance the entire experience.

Unsurprisingly, dining at Entre Cielos is all about embracing local Argentine traditions with added modern influences. Surrounded by views of the Andes Mountains and vineyards, Katharina Bistro underscores regional flavours with notable flashes of international inspiration. Close by, the Beef Club serves a variety of local meats, seasonal vegetables and fresh fish, accompanied by the resort's own wine labels, including the much-lauded Gran Marantal.

For those who wish to balance indulgence with rejuvenation, the resort's swimming pool sits alongside the Vita Parcours outdoor fitness course. A 1.6-kilometre terrain comprising workout checkpoints and a stretching zone, it shares views of both the Andes and surrounding vineyards.

And so, as the ultimate destination for rest and outstanding vinous indulgence, Entre Cielos fuses modern comforts, ancient rituals and award-winning wines to create a world-class sanctuary for body, soul, spirit and palate. BHS

DANIELA WÄGER-SPREAFICO, DAVID WÄGER AND CÉCILE ADAM

'Entre Cielos' translates as 'between heavens', and there are few locations where this description could better suit the destination. Back in 2009 Daniela Wäger-Spreafico, David Wäger and Cécile Adam fell in love with the city of Mendoza, its vineyards and its people. Inspired to build and launch a top-flight vinous holiday destination, the group pooled their savings and purchased an eight-hectare plot with sweeping views of the Andes. Aiming to create the continent's first authentic hammam spa with a luxury wine-hotel, the trio founded this ground-breaking South American retreat in the middle of the Mendoza countryside. The resort has since become a Mecca for sophisticated globetrotters whose fascination with good food and wine is matched only by their love of the outdoors. If there is one place in the world that seamlessly blends the two while entertaining guests under sapphire-blue Argentinian skies, it's Entre Cielos.

HAMANASI ADVENTURE AND DIVE RESORT

Hopkins, Belize

Strictly speaking, there are just two types of tropical holidays: those spent relaxing on the beach and touring local attractions; and those spent primarily underwater, exploring coves, coral and shipwrecks. While land-based adventures are varied, universally popular and relatively straightforward to organize, diving trips tend to present very different propositions. For one thing, committed divers are often intent on spending the majority of their holiday beneath the waves, leaving their less enthusiastic partners and companions waiting around for them on dry land. But what if a destination could persuasively combine these two very different interests? As one of the world's leading dive and adventure resorts, Hamanasi provides a happy medium for both groups.

Located south of Hopkins between the Maya Mountains and the Caribbean Sea, this quiet boutique hotel looks out onto a typically picturesque beachfront. Locally staffed, sustainably built and environmentally friendly from the ground up, Hamanasi is an outstanding place from which to explore the best of Belize. Situated on 18 hectares of land, of which 20 are set aside as a private nature reserve, the resort features four distinct eco-zones: Beachfront; Littoral Forest; Pond; and Savannah. At its heart, the Great House is reminiscent of an ancient plantation home and is blessed with a freshwater infinity pool and jaw-dropping rooftop views.

Close by, the spacious, minimalist Beachfront rooms boast mahogany beds and floor-to-ceiling windows looking out

The rarest combination of warm hospitality, limitless on-land excursions and extraordinary diving on the world's second-largest barrier reef.

28 ROOMS BAR BEACH GYM HELIPAD POOL RESTAURANT SPA

HAMANASI ADVENTURE AND DIVE RESORT, SITTEE RIVER ROAD, HOPKINS VILLAGE, STANN CREEK, BELIZE
1-844-235-4930 | INFO@HAMANASI.COM | WWW.HAMANASI.COM

over the shore. Bedecked with flashes of Toucan-inspired colours, tiled terracotta floors and unfussy yet comfortable furniture, both these and the family-friendly Beachfront Plus rooms exit onto ocean-facing verandas. And for those seeking the ultimate in privacy, the Littoral Forest hides a mini-village of luxury treehouses sitting 3.5 metres above the ground amid the rainforest canopy. With hand-carved four-poster beds, spacious living areas, twin rain showers and brightly coloured décor, these air-conditioned treetop retreats provide bird's-eye views without interruptions.

Down below, the resort's exhaustive activity list is sufficiently varied to appeal to the majority of tastes. Ideal for guests who are keen to explore Belize's marine and mainland activities, or for couples and groups with diverging interests, the Reef and Rainforest package combines several mix-and-match options. Home to three of the Caribbean's four atolls, Belize Barrier Reef's extensive ecosystem is the largest such reserve in the country, and is the place to spot sea turtles, moray eels, barracudas, dolphins, southern stingrays and several species of shark. Indeed, the snorkelling, diving and reef-exploration

trips open up an underwater world of such beauty and diversity, it makes everyday life on terra firma seem hopelessly prosaic.

Fortunately, however, a wide range of on-land distractions help counter the balance. With jungle treks, tropical birding walks and archaeological hikes in search of ancient Mayan settlements available, Hamanasi's activity packages open up Belize to the full spectrum of visitors. Indeed, it is the archetypal destination for people of all abilities and tastes. This is beautiful Belize at its most glorious, and it's worth discovering right now. BHS

ECHO VALLEY RANCH AND SPA

British Columbia, Canada

Swiss Alpine-style lodge meets Thai spa and the Canadian outdoors in this heterogeneous rural corner of British Columbia's Fraser Valley.

Quite possibly the most overused cliché in travel writing, the expression a 'land of contrasts' has become as tired and anodyne as 'exotic flavours' and 'oasis of calm'. The difficulty here, however, is that there are few more suitable descriptions to capture the essence of Echo Valley Ranch. Located deep in British Columbia's Cariboo mountain range, just a few hours north-east of Vancouver, the resort offers traditional Western-style rustic wood cabins and a commendably authentic Thai-inspired spa complex.

Establishing the business two decades ago, owners Nan and Norm did so with a dual purpose: first, to provide a luxury retreat for holidaymakers seeking respite, relaxation and exploration; and, second, to underpin this with uncompromising environmental awareness and values. It is hard to overstate just how successful Echo Valley has been in achieving these objectives. A gold star member of Green Tourism Canada, the ranch prioritizes both the replenishment of the minerals and nutrients it takes out of the land and the reduction of energy consumption. From water-efficient plumbing and energy-smart lighting, to tree-planting opportunities for guests and a geothermal heating system for the spa, its sustainability credentials are unparalleled in a resort of this calibre. And such commitment is also evident in the menus; with guests and staff actively encouraged to enjoy meals together at the family table in the open-plan kitchen, it makes for a jovial, relaxed atmosphere. Laying on Western-style barbeques and Eastern-themed Thai nights, the chefs prepare farm-fresh meals as part of Norm's self-devised '100-Metre Diet'. And in using only organic, local ingredients – many of them grown or raised on the ranch itself – the kitchen team helps diners do away with any latent food guilt.

Meanwhile, representing the heart

18 ROOMS/CABINS FITNESS CENTRE **PET-FRIENDLY** POOL **RESTAURANT** SPA

ECHO VALLEY RANCH AND SPA, 10635 JESMOND RD, CLINTON, BC V0K 1K0, CANADA
+1800 253 8831 | INFO@EVRANCH.COM | WWW.EVRANCH.COM

NORM AND NAN DOVE

Awed by its beauty and overriding sense of spirituality, Norm and Nan fell in love with the Echo Valley area almost immediately after visiting it for the first time. In founding a unique, eco-friendly resort in the Canadian wilderness, the couple fulfilled a long-held dream to create a retreat that prioritizes both people and planet. From happy staff, sustainable water sources and energy-efficient buildings, to local food suppliers and contented livestock grazing in the fields, environmental responsibility is permanently top of the agenda. Heading up a multinational ranch team, Nan and Norm encourage compassion, tolerance, peace and friendliness as the underlying principles of their corporate philosophy. Unsurprisingly, the guests also sense such qualities the moment they arrive, and are swiftly embraced as part of the Echo Valley family.

of Echo Valley, Dove Lodge incorporates the dining and games areas, while the Premium Rooms of Lookout Lodge yield spectacular views of Mount Bowman. As the resort's flagship accommodation, the Royal Suite also includes a wellness bathroom and private outdoor seating area. Unsurprisingly there are panoramic vistas of the entire estate from every angle, and with riding, fly-fishing, hiking, mountain-biking and white-water rafting all available, it is harder than you'd think to sit around doing nothing; the Ranch is that kind of resort, and contradictions are commonplace.

A case in point is the Baan Thai Spa. Fusing traditional Thai architecture with Western influences, the crafted curved roofs are twinned with advanced technology to ensure a cutting-edge approach to relaxation. Inside, the aroma of specially blended oils, herbs and spices hints at the specialized treatments available from the team of professional therapists. Likewise, the Sabai Sabai suite is furnished with hand-crafted beds and equipped with a mountain-mist herbal steam-bath and jet-shower. From Thai yoga and beauty services to hair-and-scalp therapies and full-body massages, the spa complex is the only one of its kind in North America.

It is this uniqueness and the contrasting nature of the resort as a whole that makes it remarkable; indeed, Echo Valley Ranch and Spa is a concept that arguably works better because of its contradictions. From the Swiss-style ski lodge appearance to the Little House on the Prairie terrain, and the multicultural personality to the sublime Thai spa, its character is wonderfully, addictively incongruous. Surprising and refreshing; relaxing and exhausting; fun and confounding, it is the archetypal East-meets-West paradox. BHS

DRAKE BAY GETAWAY RESORT

Osa Peninsula, Costa Rica

Aimed primarily at courting couples and adventure-seekers, these private eco-lodges specialize in the provision of fine food, wildlife tours and universal access to irresistibly dramatic views.

5 PRIVATE CABINS   BEACH   GOURMET FOOD   IN-ROOM BODY MASSAGE

OCEAN AND RAINFOREST VIEWS   ORTHOPAEDIC BEDS   RESTAURANT

DRAKE BAY GETAWAY RESORT, OSA PENINSULA, COSTA RICA
+ 506 6003-7253 | INFO@DRAKEBAYGETAWAY.COM | WWW.DRAKEBAYGETAWAY.COM

BOUTIQUE
HOTEL
SELECTION   38   AMERICAS & CARIBBEAN

As the most exclusive cabin in the resort, Bromeliad is a spacious, rustic luxury escape with a large balcony overlooking the sea, the Drake Bay jungle and Corcovado National Park.

A boutique beach destination designed with romance in mind, Drake Bay Getaway's accommodation comprises five private cabins, each with a King-size bed, twin rain showers and open-air decks. Owners Yens and Patrick, who relocated from Seattle to launch their holiday business in the heart of Costa Rica's Osa Peninsula, designed the resort with sustainable values top of the agenda.

Built using teak from a specially selected Costa Rican production farm, the cabins themselves were engineered with ingenious passive cooling technology in place of conventional air conditioning. Situated closest to the beach and blessed with the most private deck of all, Heliconia is surrounded by the eponymous plant and associated wildlife. During the rainy season a burst of colour appears around the cabin, with birds and butterflies attracted to the flowers' distinctive red-and-yellow petals. Nearby, and with a large window and balcony facing the mountains, the Orchid was designed as the perfect location from which to witness a Costa Rican sunrise.

Meanwhile, occupying the first floor of the highest point in the Drake Bay Getaway Resort, Lantana looks out over the Corcovado National Park and the Pacific Ocean. With the entire second floor dedicated to 'Passion', the building's unique position affords exceptional views of the surrounding bay, jungle and national park.

Finally, as the most exclusive cabin in the resort, Bromeliad is a spacious, rustic luxury escape with a large balcony

YENS STELLER AND PATRICK LUDWIG

overlooking the sea, the Drake Bay jungle and Corcovado National Park. It simply does not get better than this.

Eager for guests to immerse themselves in the beauty of the surrounding area, Yens and Patrick actively encourage participation in the wide variety of world-class tours on offer. Between diving at Caño Island, kayaking through the mangrove forests and whale-watching* in the bay below, the only challenge is choosing which to prioritize. That aside, with arguably the most biodiverse environment of its kind on Earth, it's nigh impossible to resist exploring Corcovado National Park. Playing host to sloths, snakes, monkeys, tapirs and hundreds of species of birds, it will complete a list of must-see creatures quicker than a trip to local zoo back home.

When hunger finally, inevitably, catches up, Yens' and Patrick's legendary all-inclusive visitor package is akin to

*August to October

being at home but with an upgrade to first class. Inspired by traditional Costa Rican cooking techniques, the kitchen team employs fresh ingredients to prepare the menus for breakfast, lunch and dinner. Using produce from local sources including the resort's own organic vegetable garden, the chefs encourage guests to discover the full range of both Latin American and international fusion cuisine. And with an impossibly tempting range of speciality coffees available, it is hard to find a reason to venture outside again.

Fittingly, given its suitability for honeymooners, the facilities at Drake Bay Getaway Resort are notably geared towards couples. So, although a babysitting service and childcare are available, it is unlikely that your stay will be interrupted by the pitter-patter of demanding, albeit tiny, feet; worth remembering the next time the prospect of a romantic getaway becomes more than a mere pipe dream . . . **BHS**

Before moving to Costa Rica in 2013, Yens and Patrick worked for several cutting-edge technology companies in Seattle, USA. Keen to make major changes in their lives, they abandoned their tech careers to take on the new challenge of building a boutique resort in one of the most remote locations on the planet. The result is a world-class destination that has been constructed according to the strictest principles of environmentally friendly development. Built using 80% recyclable materials – including some of the finest sustainably harvested teak wood in Costa Rica – Drake Bay Getaway's mission is to become a leading global destination for eco-tourism. Focusing on providing the best personalized services with the least impact to the environment, Yens and Patrick are committed to developing and expanding green practices within the resort.

THE LIBRARY HOTEL

New York City, New York

Situated in an almost implausibly convenient location between Grand Central Station and Times Square, this gem in America's artistic crown presents a truly unique guest experience.

60 ROOMS   COMPLIMENTARY CONTINENTAL BREAKFAST

COMPLIMENTARY WINE-AND-CHEESE RECEPTION   ROOF TERRACE

THE LIBRARY HOTEL, 299 MADISON AVENUE, NEW YORK, NY 10017, USA
+1 212 983 4500 | RESERVATIONS@LIBRARYHOTEL.COM | WWW.LIBRARYHOTEL.COM

BOUTIQUE HOTEL SELECTION   42   AMERICAS & CARIBBEAN

Justifiably regarded as one of the Big Apple's most revered boutique establishments, the Library Hotel pays homage to an enduring concept of modern society. Laid out and arranged in accordance with the Dewey Decimal System, the 10 guestroom floors honour the categories of Melvil Dewey's eponymous 19th-century library classification structure.

Exclusive, if not esoteric, the hotel is understandably a Mecca for travel-hungry bibliophiles. Each of the 60 individually designed rooms boasts a collection of books and art relating to the specific category to which it belongs: from literature, technology, general knowledge, religion and social sciences, to languages, philosophy, history, maths-and-science and the arts – it's all there.

Showcasing a mythical source of inspiration and respite from the buzz and the crowds of the outside world, the 6,000 titles themselves are arranged throughout the hotel. Indeed, the arresting beauty of the heavily laden shelves is matched only by the ambition with which the concept was conceived. However, it is not all about the books, as hospitality and conviviality are very much an integral part of the experience. The complimentary continental breakfasts are much appreciated by regulars and first-time visitors alike. Of an evening, after an energetic day's sightseeing around the city, it's hard to resist unwinding at the wine-and-cheese reception, which is also on the house. Later, enjoy highly commendable fare in the laidback setting of the in-house Madison & Vine restaurant, before retiring upstairs for literary-themed cocktails at the Bookmarks bar. From this rooftop base – Hemingway in hand and iconic Manhattan skyline in the background – it is hard to feel more like an indigenous New Yorker.

Incidentally, if the thought of sitting around reading all week is a guilt trip waiting to happen, fear not. Guests are afforded entry to several of the city's fabled sports clubs during their stay. In the City That Never Sleeps, exercising body and mind has never been so engaging. **BHS**

MEET THE VISIONARY

HENRY KALLAN

When Henry Kallan emigrated to the Big Apple from the former Czechoslovakia at 21 years of age, his hospitality debut as a busboy proved as inspiring as it was relentless. Working his way up through various hotel companies over the years, by 27 he had become the city's youngest general manager. In 2000, following the success of Hotel Elysee, Casablanca Hotel and Hotel Giraffe, he opened the Library Hotel as a the fourth jewel of the Library Hotel Collection which is now seven-strong with the 2017 launch of Hotel X Toronto. Inspired by the local culture and the nearby New York Public Library, Henry designed a book lovers' paradise and the namesake of the Library Hotel Collection. He is tirelessly passionate about creating outstanding guest experiences, leading the company to have earned the highest guest satisfaction ratings of any luxury hotel brand in the world.

O:LIVE
BOUTIQUE HOTEL

San Juan, Puerto Rico

Born of its founders' experiences travelling the world, this stunning retreat pens a heartfelt love letter to the Mediterranean, writ large upon a Caribbean canvas.

14 ROOMS AND 1 HONEYMOON SUITE   BAR   PLUNGE POOL   RESTAURANT   ROOFTOP VIEWS

O:LIVE BOUTIQUE HOTEL, AGUADILLA STREET #55, CONDADO, 00907, PUERTO RICO
+787 705 9994 | RESERVATIONS@OLIVEBOUTIQUEHOTEL.COM | WWW.OLIVEBOUTIQUEHOTEL.COM

BOUTIQUE
HOTEL    45   AMERICAS & CARIBBEAN
SELECTION

It is a widely accepted verity that travel broadens the mind, although the extent to which this is true probably depends less on how far one goes and more on the eventual destination. Having extensively explored and fallen in love with Europe – even marrying in Sorrento – Loisse Herger and Fernando Dávila were already well-qualified to found a Mediterranean-influenced boutique establishment on the other side of the world.

Following the triumph of their first foray in hospitality, when they took over the successful Hostería del Mar, the couple launched O:live in 2012. In the intervening years they have channelled their enthusiasm into this rustic, luxurious hotel situated close to the busy-but-beautiful Laguna del Condado in Puerto Rico's capital, San Juan.

Decorated in divergent styles, each

of the hotel's hallways is festooned with photographs, souvenirs and artwork collected during the duo's global adventures: where one such hall accents the Provençal style, others flaunt the colours, tones and influences of Spain and Italy. Indeed, behind every detail in O:live lies a story of the couple's world travels, producing a timeless look using old-style furnishings sourced from specialist curators and collectors.

Similarly, a climb up to the rooftop is rewarded with a fashionable wrought iron-and-hardwood sun terrace which affords spectacular views of the windswept lagoon below.

Meanwhile, the ultra-chic Sage restaurant evokes the sights and aromas of the Iberian Peninsula. Showcasing ingenious fusions of Mediterranean textures and flavours, Chef Mario Pagán's menu

employs local flavours such as papaya and mango to create new variations of classic steakhouse fare. Internationally recognized as one of the area's top chefs, Mario possesses a playful knack for inventiveness, complementing his dishes with bread accompanied by pork crackling crust, and serving quirky condiments like guava ketchup. It is a refreshing take on perennially popular dishes and it makes for a beguiling gourmet experience.

Spread throughout the hotel, O:live's 15 suites are inspired by 'l'art de vivre' and present a unique exemplar of relaxed luxury. Spacious and beautifully appointed, they vary in size from 31.5 to 61 square metres and boast rainfall showers and queen-size beds. Understandably, given the hosts' dominant source of inspiration here, three deserve special mention: equipped with see-through

LOISSE HERGER AND FERNANDO DÁVILA

Having long held a candle for the miracles of Mediterranean life, committed globetrotters Loisse and Fernando have built a growing business based around their travel experiences. After an aunt bestowed upon them as a wedding gift her beloved Puerto Rican guest house, Hostería del Mar, the newlyweds discovered their inner hoteliers. Following the success of this first foray into hospitality, they were spurred on to launch O:live Boutique Hotel, in 2012. In the intervening years, the business has picked up a significant number of admirers and awards, highlighting the couple's natural affinity with the world of travel from the other side of the reception desk. Currently hard at work renovating a neighbouring building, they are living their dream in real time. And soon, Puerto Rico's window to the Mediterranean will be just a little bit bigger.

showers, a separate dining area for two and either a terrace or veranda, both the Mediterranean and Lagoon View Mediterranean suites are capable of mentally transporting guests back over the pond to mainland Europe. Flanked by Spanish tiles and restored European woods while gazing out over San Juan's distinctive Caribbean metropolis, occupants are treated to a fascinating juxtaposition of cultures. And as the largest, most decadent suite, the Grand Cru represents an exquisite honeymoon hideaway with an extended living area and extra-large outdoor patio.

However, the characteristic that sets this place apart from all other hotels is its hosts' relentless drive to discover new inspirations with which to influence and improve the O:live experience. For despite apparently settling down to run their new venture, Loisse and Fernando are more focused than ever on identifying alternative destinations and places of interest in their quest to bring different dimensions to the O:live brand. Whereas the refresh and refurbishment of most properties tends to be both cyclical and all-encompassing, O:live's constantly evolving design depends on where the couple travels to next. As a consequence, this enchanting hotel will quite possibly never appear the same on any two occasions.

The Indian novelist Anita Desai once wrote: 'Wherever you go becomes a part of you, somehow.' It is especially true for this particular boutique establishment, which is all the better for where its founders have been and where they intend to visit in the years ahead. **BHS**

MAISON BLANC BLEU

Saint-Barthélemy, French West Indies

A soulful, luxuriously appointed retreat located close to St Barth's historic capital, Gustavia, this sublime exclusive-use villa exemplifies life in the West Indies.

With a population of less than 10,000, Saint-Barthélemy is a French-speaking island more commonly referred to as St Barth. Despite being famous for its white-sand beaches, fine dining and chic hotels, this arid volcanic rock, just 21 square kilometres, is still one of the quieter islands in the Caribbean.

Perched above the quartier of Lurin, not far from Gustavia, Maison Blanc Bleu symbolizes the very essence of the St Barth lifestyle. Laid back, luxurious and with boundless sea views, it is perfect both for families and large groups.

Setting the tone for the rest of the accommodation, the spacious, comfortable, minimalist Master Suite occupies an entire level on its own. In addition to the five remaining ensuite bedrooms,

6 BEDROOMS   BREAKFAST BAR   BUBBLE POOL   FITNESS GYM   LARGE SUNDECK

PRIVATE TENNIS COURT   SHADED AL FRESCO DINING AREA   SWIMMING POOL WITH SEA VIEW

MAISON BLANC BLEU, SAINT-BARTHÉLEMY, FRENCH WEST INDIES
+44 208 672 7040 | INFO@MYPRIVATEVILLAS.COM | WWW.SIBARTH.COM

As a destination in its own right, St Barth is widely considered among most unusual of the French West Indies, as well as the most rewarding.

the floor below incorporates the state-of-the-art kitchen and breakfast bar, flanked by immaculate white-leather tall chairs. Extending out into a large indoor/outdoor living area, the entire space is designed for socializing and relaxing, and is ideal for private celebrations or simply retreating from the stresses of everyday life.

Outside, Maison Blanc Bleu's ocean-facing swimming pool forms the centrepiece of the expansive grounds, while the villa's tennis court represents a notable addition that no other private accommodation on the island is able to match.

Of course, if the instinct to explore begins to supplant the need to do nothing, there is plenty to see and do in the surrounding area. As a destination in its own right, St Barth is widely considered among most unusual of the French West Indies, as well as the most rewarding. With its melting pot of French and Swedish colonial history, stunning beaches and tropical scenery, it is a popular holiday spot for those seeking rest and recuperation. However, despite its reputation as a Mecca for celebrities and the well-heeled elite, the island remains as unpretentious and

unspoiled as it is warm and welcoming. Having managed to conserve its charm and simplicity in the face of recent modernization and a significant increase in wealth, Gustavia still teems with heritage, culture and charm. By way of illustration, a walk along the waterfront yields a variety of glaring, if pleasing, incongruities, all of which contribute to the town's allure. Irresistible activities include people-watching from the abundant local cafés and gazing out at the modern, frequently grandiose mega-yachts berthed in the bay. Indeed, the very beauty of St Barth lies in its ubiquitous blends of classic and contemporary, old and new.

Adding to its appeal are the numerous world-class eateries. With over 80 restaurants serving everything from French and Asian cuisine to Italian and Creole dishes, the island's gastronomic quarter has become something of a recognized attraction in itself.

It is therefore not too surprising that a palpably sporty atmosphere hovers over the island, perhaps as part of a conscious effort to cancel out the effects of all that rich food. With everything from outdoor Hatha yoga, Judo and Taekwondo, to basketball, archery, sailing, scuba-diving and jet-skiing, there is a variety of activities on the go.

All of this – in addition to St Barth's 14 exceptional beaches – makes Maison Blanc Bleu a uniquely attractive prospect for a Caribbean holiday. Blessed with a spacious, luxurious interior, extensive grounds, private tennis court, stunning pool and eye-widening ocean views, it is probably the most exclusive villa destination on the island. BHS

FOND DOUX PLANTATION AND RESORT

Soufrière, St Lucia

Located in the heart of a 250-year-old cacao plantation, this eco-friendly resort is famed for its luxury cottages, authentic Caribbean experience and, above all, its chocolate.

Whisky and wine aside, there are few food-and-drink attractions that can captivate visitors in the same way chocolate seduces people of all nationalities, backgrounds, cultures and tastes. With its broad varieties, unmistakable texture and near-universal appeal it is arguably one of the most popular foodstuffs on the planet. Consequently, this makes Fond Doux – a historic source of chocolate's key ingredient – a deliciously tempting tourist destination.

Located on St Lucia's west coast and luring visitors from around the world, this ancient but still-operational plantation forms the backdrop to a luxury eco-resort. Featuring 15 traditional-style French Colonial cottages overlooking white-sand beaches and coral reefs, the location lends itself equally to families, groups, individuals and couples. Once slated for demolition, the century-old wooden buildings were dismantled and relocated to the resort before being comprehensively restored and reopened as guest accommodation. Unique in their own right, they lie hidden amid tropical cocoa groves in the shadow of the coastal peaks of the nearby Piton Mountains.

Sleeping between two and four guests, each cottage is equipped with luxury bathroom, king-size bed and, in some cases, self-catering kitchen and a balcony or patio. Sharing its space with fruit trees and Day-Glo-coloured birds of paradise, the stand-out Honeymoon Suite's outdoor rainforest

15 COTTAGES   BAR   ORGANIC SPA   THREE SWIMMING POOLS   TWO ON-SITE RESTAURANTS   WALKING TOURS

FOND DOUX PLANTATION AND RESORT, P.O. BOX 250, ST LUCIA
+1 758 459 7545 | INFO@FONDDOUXESTATE.COM | WWW.FONDDOUXESTATE.COM

shower and private plunge pool make it ideal for a romantic break in merciful isolation from the usual tourist hotspots.

Outside the resort, the jungles, waterfalls and the Caribbean's only 'drive-in volcano', Sulphur Springs, provide the quintessential tropical experience infused with St Lucia's typical warmth, hospitality and charm.

Meanwhile, Fond Doux's twin restaurants serve both traditional and international cuisine, much of it prepared with ingredients sourced from within the resort itself. A significant component of the St Lucian culture, food and the techniques required for its preparation represent a popular *divertissement* for both locals and guests. And with the Mama La Terre Spa's extensive inventory of treatments – not to mention the infinite outdoor playground for snorkelling, scuba diving and hiking – Fond Doux focuses on the restorative powers of nature to help guests wind down a couple of gears.

That said, it is perhaps the resort's capacity as a Mecca for cacao fans that ultimately makes it so attractive. With guided tours of the harvesting, drying and grinding processes, it is as educational as it is entertaining and seductive.

For true connoisseurs, a visit to a genuine working cacao plantation is akin to a music fan's pilgrimage to their hero's birthplace. In this regard, Fond Doux is to chocoholics what Graceland represents to Elvis fans. BHS

Featuring 15 traditional-style French Colonial cottages overlooking white-sand beaches and coral reefs, the location lends itself equally to families, groups, individuals and couples.

OVER YONDER CAY

The Bahamas

Live the life of an eco-friendly global superstar on this exclusive-use Caribbean island equipped with luxury villas, private yacht and renewable energy sources.

4 VILLAS CHILD-FRIENDLY ECO-FRIENDLY GAMES ROOM GYM INFINITY POOLS
NINE-HOLE GOLF COURSE PRIVATE YACHT SPA TENNIS COURT

OVER YONDER CAY, THE EXUMAS, BAHAMAS
+44 208 672 7040 | INFO@MYPRIVATEVILLAS.COM | WWW.OVERYONDERCAY.COM

BOUTIQUE
HOTEL   55   AMERICAS & CARIBBEAN
SELECTION

If the dream of an alternative existence has ever manifested itself in a reverie about being fabulously, preternaturally wealthy, the chances are it included ownership of a tropical island. With unlimited resources at one's disposal, it is hard to predict just how exceptional the ultimate private getaway could be; marinas, yachts, wildlife, waterfalls and ivory-coloured beaches would all presumably come as standard. But what about the sprawling palatial accommodation, teeming coral reefs, floodlit tennis courts and private golf course? Would they all be included too? Fortunately, the availability of Over Yonder Cay as a fully staffed A-grade eco-friendly retreat eliminates any such uncertainty.

Situated in the Exuma Chain, 400 kilometres south-east of Florida, this former fishing-outpost-turned-luxury-bolthole represents the embodiment of barefooted decadence. Its four expansive private villas, each in a secluded location with private beach, accommodate a total of 28 guests. Of these, Meridian House is the largest, its prodigious footprint sitting aloft near the middle of the island.

Close by, West Sands overlooks Whale Bone Beach and sleeps eight guests in four bedrooms, while East Cove's elevated position and wraparound balconies afford exceptional views over the Exuma Sound. Meanwhile, from its more isolated location on the southernmost tip of the island, South Point's see-through shallow waters

leave guests with little alternative but to take the plunge. And with a variety of water sports, sunset sailing cruises, diving excursions, jet skis and snorkelling safaris on offer, there is more than sufficient incentive to remain submerged. Indeed, with its own shallow reef, deep caves, abundant marine life and the occasional sunken ship to explore, the underwater adventures here are as exciting as those on land.

And when hunger inevitably drags everyone back to shore, the island's team of chefs serve up superb refreshments, often prepared using produce gathered by guests themselves during the optional game-fishing expeditions on the open ocean. Meanwhile, Over Yonder Cay's

deep-water dock can accommodate vessels of up to 55 metres in length, including Tenacious, the island's very own sailing yacht. With space for eight people to enjoy guided tours around the neighbouring archipelago, this 35-metre sloop provides an effortlessly fashionable introduction to the crystalline shoreline and attendant coral reef.

However, the reign of the traditional internal-combustion engine pretty much ends there. Powered by a state-of-the-art renewable energy system including three wind turbines and a solar field of more than 2,000 photovoltaic panels, the entire island is a self-generating beacon of the sustainable-energy ideal. At its heart lies a battery-based system capable of storing up to two days' power, with excess production automatically diverted to produce water for drinking and irrigation, and to heat the pools and Jacuzzis. With its 96% renewable energy penetration, this Bahamian idyll literally lights the way for others to follow.

Aided by a genial, highly experienced team of guides, instructors and spa therapists – not to mention party-friendly facilities including DJ station, dance floor and bar – Over Yonder Cay is a rock-star's retreat for large families and groups. As a pioneering, environmentally conscious resort, it is hard to beat; as an ultra-exclusive, private luxury holiday destination, it is unparalleled. This really is the dream. BHS

Powered by a state-of-the-art renewable energy system including three wind turbines and a solar field of more than 2,000 photovoltaic panels, the entire island is a self-generating beacon of the sustainable-energy ideal.

 **JDB** FINE HOTELS & RESORTS

 THE *hush*™ COLLECTION

AN UNSURPASSED COLLECTION OF THE FINEST AND MOST UNIQUE PROPERTIES

For more than 30 years JDB Fine Hotels
& Resorts has represented the best
hotels and resorts in Italy, France and
Spain to meet the needs of discerning
travelers. Recently, the Hush Collection has
been added to our portfolio with its outstanding
Caribbean and Latin American boutique hotels
and resorts.

jdbhotels.com | thehushcollection.com

ASIA

BHS

THE OLYMPIAN HONG KONG

Kowloon, Hong Kong

A fresh addition to the lively cultural quarter of West Kowloon, The Olympian Hong Kong combines the space, comfort and facilities of a much larger hotel with the bespoke service and charm of a boutique establishment.

32 ROOMS   BUTLER SERVICE   FITNESS CENTRE   INTERCONNECTED FAMILY ROOMS   STUNNING VIEWS

THE OLYMPIAN HONG KONG, 18 HOI FAI ROAD, WEST KOWLOON, HONG KONG
+852 3199 8888 | INFO@THEOLYMPIANHOTEL.COM | WWW.THEOLYMPIANHOTEL.COM

BOUTIQUE
HOTEL    62   ASIA
SELECTION

With all 32 rooms and suites positioned on the same floor, The Olympian Hong Kong enjoys the feel of a private residence. Launching in March 2016, this latest development by Hong Kong-based Sino Hotels presents a welcome outpost with plenty of de-stress potential in this relentlessly energetic city.

Complemented by floor-to-ceiling windows with attendant views, the spacious Deluxe Olympian rooms are designed for guests seeking the comforts of home with the refinement of a modern hotel. The Grand Harbour View accommodation, meanwhile, achieves considerably more than merely living up to its eponymous remit; limited to just 11 rooms, these blend state-of-the-

art facilities with generous living space to create a sophisticated, comfortable residential retreat. And as the ultimate rooms for special occasions, each of the eight Olympian Suites provides 75 square metres of living space and panoramic views of Victoria Harbour and that seminal tower-studded skyline.

Somewhat fortuitously, the hotel's launch has coincided with the introduction of a weekly LED light display which takes place on two façades of the International Finance Centre across the harbour. Employing up to 50,000 square metres of lights, the record-breaking spectacle makes the rest of this famously radiant city appear like it's suffered a power cut.

And when the opportunity arises to explore a little farther than the bedroom,

West Kowloon represents the archetypal tourist-friendly neighbourhood, despite being as vibrant and densely populated as the rest of Hong Kong. Known as the Golden Circle, the area offers diverse shopping and dining scenes, from the refinement of Michelin-Starred restaurants to the addictive chaos of Temple Street Night Market, and everything in between. It also promotes compellingly easy access via the subway to the city's central district on Hong Kong Island.

Flawlessly located in its epicentre and enhanced by thoughtful touches including extended-stay packages and 24-hour gymnasium access, The Olympian Hong Kong offers a refreshingly imaginative approach in this vibrant hub of business, art and culture. **BHS**

SUMMERTIME VILLA

Goa, India

Celebrate all that is great about Goa and enjoy peace and privacy in this exclusive-use hilltop home that demands to be filled with family and friends.

3 SUITES POOL ROOFTOP VIEWS

SUMMERTIME VILLA, 2/286 BOA VIAGEM ROAD, NAIKAVADDO, CALANGUTE, GOA 403516, INDIA
INFO@SUMMERTIMEGOA.COM | WWW.SUMMERTIMEGOA.COM

Built in contemporary Asian style, the villa boasts large living spaces and extensive, verdant grounds with panoramic views.

Spacious; charming; warm; welcoming: four words that perfectly summarize Summertime. Aimed at tourists seeking a relaxed and sumptuous setting for entertaining friends and celebrating special occasions, this sprawling, fully serviced establishment presents a unique holiday proposition. Located near the lively villages of Calangute and Candolim, the three-bedroom property enjoys easy access to restaurants, beaches and night markets, and yet remains mercifully isolated from all of them.

Built in contemporary Asian style, the villa boasts large living spaces and extensive, verdant grounds with panoramic views.

The air-conditioned suites – Koi, Coral and Sunflower – are similar to each other in size but offer unique, bespoke highlights. More like traditional master bedrooms than standard or even deluxe accommodation, each is large and luxurious enough to feel like a self-contained apartment. Located on the ground floor, just off the dining veranda, Koi showcases a super-size Italian marble bathtub, tall French windows and direct access to a private garden. Upstairs, on the first floor, the Coral Suite's four-poster bed and cavernous bathroom make it a couples' favourite; and although the separate beds of the Sunflower Suite – which may be joined together to create an enormous double – are complemented by a dressing area and spacious bathroom, its real defining feature is the fabulous view over the swimming pool and nearby gardens.

However, despite these attractions, it is the villa's living area and indoor dining-room that represent the real draw. With its Balinese influences, tall ceilings, floor-length windows, magnificent views and unique phulkari tapestry adorning the walls, the entire space is a work of art.

Outside, overlooking the fields in the valley below, the huge infinity pool and one hectare of private landscaped gardens provide ample diversions and distractions. With fruit trees, a man-made waterfall and a colourful koi pond, Summertime's grounds are as enticing as the villa itself.

That said, there is one more hidden feature which complements, rather than diverts attention from, Summertime's amenities and facilities. Solita, a classic luxury yacht built by and belonging to the villa's owners, is available to guests for exclusive charter hire. A completely different method of exploring Goa, the 13-metre craft was designed in the classic Grand Banks style with three decks, teakwood ensuite cabins and plenty of space for socializing. From snorkelling, fishing and dolphin-watching to romantic sunset cruises, Solita showcases the island and its surrounding attractions like nothing else.

As possibly the only rental villa in Goa with private grounds of this size and diversity, and with a full complement of staff including cook, caretaker, housekeeper and gardener, Summertime is a devastatingly attractive destination for relaxing, socializing and expunging the stresses of everyday life. BHS

LA VILLA

Pondichéry, India

This beautifully restored century-old mansion has been transformed from a colonial-era home into an effortlessly chic retreat for couples and small groups of friends.

6 SUITES | BAR | INDIAN OIL MASSAGE | NO CHILDREN | PRIVATE YOGA CLASSES | POOL | RESTAURANT

LA VILLA, 11 SURCOUF STREET, PONDICHÉRY, 605001, INDIA
91 413 2338555 | LAVILLA@LAVILLA.IN | WWW.LAVILLAPONDICHERRY.COM
Architects: T. Trigala, Y. Lesprit, Paris | Photography: Mia Studio, Auroville

BOUTIQUE HOTEL SELECTION — 66 — ASIA

Meticulously renovated, the six-suite hotel is located in the heart of the French quarter, just a short walk from the town's famous promenade. Showcasing distinctive furnishings, teakwood floors, new-age lamps and sleek white bathrooms, the suites epitomize sublime design. Individually styled and equipped with rain showers and either a balcony or private terrace, each room is laid out in a pleasingly unconventional style with at least one defining feature; from the wooden semi-enclosure of Escale à Pondichéry and the long, narrow corridor of India Song, to the integrated canopy above the vast bed in Bridge to Heaven, no two rooms are the same. Even apparent twins North Side Story and its southern sister both benefit, by definition, from different views.

Meanwhile, as a novel alternative to generic indoor breakfast and dining-rooms, the restaurant is shared between the front porch and the courtyard. Wooden tables and wicker chairs sit amid indigenous plants and ancient trees, and the overriding feeling is one of friendliness and familiarity; indeed, were it not for the warm weather and fellow guests murmuring over the menu a few metres away, it rather lends the impression of savouring dinner in the garden at home. It is a pleasant, reassuring feeling, and a welcome change from the sterile character-vacuums of the international chain establishments. The menu itself is a refreshingly intelligible page of salads, steaks, curries and local specialities, and the temptation to clutter it with endless variations on a similar theme has been judiciously avoided. Even the vegetarian options are highlighted in a bold green typeface, and the end result is one of merciful simplicity.

Come morning, break-fast may be taken in the suite, beside the pool or in the front garden, and a colourful spread of freshly prepared items sets the tone for the forthcoming day of exploration and relaxation.

The evening sitting, on the other hand, is a somewhat more formal experience and all the better for it. With candlelit tables and seasonal dishes rich in colour and flavour garnishing the finest porcelain and silver tableware, La Villa's sublime dining experience means there is never a need to venture further afield in search of taste sensation. As you would expect, such quality percolates throughout the hotel; with comfortable, contemporary suites, sumptuous food and sublime facilities, guests are implicitly encouraged to relax and soak up the inimitable South Asian atmosphere. This is just as well, for if there is one country in the world where travellers, tourists and explorers could do with periodic breaks from the mayhem, it is India. BHS

MIHIR GARH

Rajasthan, India

A bold initiative from the House of Rohet, this extraordinary, extravagant hotel rises out of the Marwar sands like a sprawling fairy-tale fortress.

9 SUITES BAR INFINITY POOL SPA

MIHIR GARH, NEAR KHANDI RAJASTHAN, HEERAWAS, RAJASTHAN, 306421, INDIA
+91 8302 706 909 | BOOKMIHIRGARH@GMAIL.COM | WWW.MIHIRGARH.COM

BOUTIQUE
HOTEL   68   ASIA
SELECTION

The equine pursuits at Mihir Garh are among the finest in the country and the indigenous Marwari horses take centre stage.

On the face of it, an isolated desert in a devilishly hot climate may not sound too tempting a prospect for the majority of tourists, many of whom prefer holidays and honeymoons to be a little more structured and conventional; formulaic, even. At Mihir Garh, such predictability simply does not exist.

The creative vision of Prince Sidharth and his wife Rashmi, the 'Fort of the Sun' was completed in 2009, the culmination of a long-held dream and years of planning. Persistently lauded by the world's travel press, this brave, ambitious design sees Rajasthan's glorious past rub shoulders with today's contemporary chic.

Perched on a sand dune and surrounded by a boundless, ruthless horizon, this palatial establishment offers a rare insight into the area's colourful rural heritage. The nine suites, each 158 square metres in size, strike a delicate balance between traditional minimalism and contemporary comfort, and the astonishing attention to detail demands closer inspection. From the Jodhpur furnishings and ornate bedrooms, to the immaculate, deeply indulgent bathrooms, there exists a pervasive, intensely satisfying aura of old versus new, history versus modernism.

Equipped with plunge pool and personal courtyard overlooking scorched shrubs and parched sands, the ground floor suites – known as Alishan – are typical features of this rather spectacular accommodation. Upstairs, the open-air Jacuzzis and

SIDHARTH AND RASHMI SINGH

private terraces of the Shandaar suites are as close as it gets to decadence in the desert. Presenting an unorthodox but ultimately welcome break from the traditional opulence of ancient palaces, the rooms here are quite possibly the most imaginative, refreshing and memorable in northern India.

Naturally, super-rich Rajasthani fare is a significant part of life at the hotel, with exquisite breakfasts and lunches freshly prepared from local ingredients. In the evenings, the Shikar dinners are a standout feature, providing a compelling route back to the days of the Raj.

Outside, the perennial heat haze signals the gradual but sustained increase in temperature throughout the day. However, such is the friendliness of the staff and the quality of the facilities, the relentless rise of the mercury fails to hamper the guest experience. Indeed, the list of outdoor activities here is so engaging, so distracting, that it threatens to divert attention away from the palace altogether. With village safaris, royal picnics, bird-watching expeditions, culinary workshops and indecently delicious barbeques under the stars, there is usually something on the go. And if solitude is key, all that is really required is a book, a bottle of water, a pair of binoculars and a borrowed bicycle.

That said, the equine pursuits at Mihir Garh are among the finest in the country and the indigenous Marwari horses take centre stage. Revered in Rajasthan like a mythical deity, these rare, magnificent creatures command legendary levels of respect and devotion. Selected for their hardiness and resilience but most famous for their beauty and grace, the breed even inspired Prince Sidharth to name his hotel's nine suites after stallions from the Rohet Stables. Unsurprisingly, the area surrounding the property is exceptionally well-suited to riding and guiding.

Delicate, detailed and clearly designed without compromise, Mihir Garh is like a living museum, a life-size tribute to Rajasthani heritage, culture, design, art and tradition. This is a place where ancient minimalism does battle with modern luxury, and both somehow emerge the victor.

If India is a land of surprises, then Mihir Garh's facilities, activities and Elysian beauty will consistently flatter and confound at every turn. Perhaps it is why Lonely Planet recently proclaimed this unforgettable, addictive celebration of luxury, culture and local tradition the Most Extraordinary Hotel in the World. **BHS**

Despite having been at the helm of some of India's most coveted establishments for more than 25 years, entrepreneurs Sidharth and Rashmi still consider Mihir Garh to be their finest work. Personally visualizing and overseeing the creation of every corner of the 'Fort of the Sun' during its development, they took exceptional care to pay homage to the arts, tradition, history and heritage of rural Rajasthan. Driven more by intuition than logic, the couple collaborated with over 100 local artists and craftsmen to create this magical hotel on the edge of the Thar Desert. Reminiscent of a bygone era and replete with decadent facilities, ornate furnishings and intricate décor, their exquisite, ground-breaking retreat is widely considered to be among the most spectacular, striking and admired of anywhere in the world.

Best Travel *for You*

Welcome to Our World.
Extraordinary Experiences
and Lasting Memories.

We personally invite you to enjoy some sensational moments with us. Let us make your travel and leisure experiences that extra bit special. We want to be there for you every step of the way, so we take the time to get to know you, your likes, your favourite things and your passions. We are a well defined team of travel experts and are constantly sourcing fresh opportunities for you, becoming more aligned to your interests as our partnership with you grows.

Contact Best Travel For You
to Get Inspired.

Call 0845 130 9022 OR
Email discover@besttravelforyou.co.uk

Simply quote World Boutique Hotels
and we will organise your requirements.

Best Travel For You is part of the Best International Group of Companies.

Best International
GROUP OF COMPANIES

Best Asset Management

 Greyfriars

SOUTH-EAST ASIA

BHS

AWARTA NUSA DUA LUXURY VILLAS AND SPA

Bali, Indonesia

This enchanting collection of spacious, immaculate private villas is the embodiment of five-star luxury and service.

14 PRIVATE RESIDENCES   24-HOUR BUTLER SERVICE   24-HOUR FITNESS CENTRE   BAR
PRIVATE DINING AREA   PRIVATE POOL   RESTAURANT   SPA

AWARTA NUSA DUA LUXURY VILLAS AND SPA, JALAN KAWASAN NUSA DUA RESORT,
ITDC COMPLEX LOT NW 2 & 3, BALI 80363, INDONESIA
+62 361 773 300 | INFO@AWARTARESORTS.COM | WWW.AWARTARESORTS.COM

BOUTIQUE
HOTEL   75   SOUTH-EAST ASIA
SELECTION

Open-plan interiors, marble floors, spa-style baths and rich furnishings are all signature villa features at Awarta Nusa Dua.

Located in a peaceful district in the south of Indonesia's most popular tourist destination, Awarta is a cleverly proportioned fusion of traditional Balinese and Chinese architecture. Developed as part of a specially curated complex of luxury hotels, shops and sporting facilities, the resort aims to inspire visitors to explore the archipelago and its many islands.

Designed with rich, bold furnishings and artwork, Awarta's 14 private residences are arranged as a self-contained village. Sympathetically constructed using traditional, sustainable materials, each property is comprehensively equipped and attended to by discreet, friendly staff. Open-plan interiors, marble floors, spa-style baths and rich furnishings are all signature features, and close proximity to the beach is a given. With large garden, own pool and an airy interior, the Private Pool Villas offer 24-hour butler service and an exclusive dining area. Further up the scale, the larger 450-square-metre, one bed Royal Orchid villa also prioritizes indoor–outdoor living and dining areas. The Two-Bedroom Private Pool Villas, on the other hand, are well-suited to families, couples and groups, adding a further bedroom and additional living space. Likewise, the

Royal Roselle increases the total size to 750 square metres and includes a private pool, dining area and 24-hour butler service.

And for the ultimate accommodation, the three-bedroom residences provide all the refinement of the other villas but with up to 950 square metres of living space.

Immediately following check-in, a prompt visit to the health spa is highly recommended. With an extensive menu of healing treatments, relaxation techniques and detox programmes, it is the essential destination for mind-and-body rejuvenation. Alongside the requisite sauna, fitness and massage facilities, the Thevana Spa offers hand-crafted treatments and homemade ingredients, while the specialist Kneipp foot therapy

is known to reduce stress and bolster the immune system; handy to know, when both of the resort's restaurants do their job so well. Preparing an encyclopaedic range of traditional Balinese and Western dishes – from extravagant breakfasts and light lunches, to afternoon snacks and intimate dinners – there is a meal or food to suit one's mood.

And when the bathing, exploring and indulging have all wrapped up for day, take a moment to sit in one of the covered daybeds and breathe in the surroundings. With extraordinary landscaping and the sweet, unmistakable scent of frangipani trees, Awarta Nusa Dua is a tropical retreat with exquisite luxury and charming Balinese hospitality at its core. BHS

DWARAKA
THE ROYAL VILLAS

Bali, Indonesia

Located near the cheerful chaos of Ubud village, these traditionally built villas present an authentic Balinese experience complemented by rural luxury and local hospitality.

Inspired by the ancient story of Lord Krishna's Kingdom, this exceptional resort incorporates the finest indigenous design into 10 lavishly appointed detached villas. Most have their own east-facing infinity pool, making breakfast at sunrise a daily joy, while the Dwaraka spa offers traditional Indonesian cleansing, toning and massage treatments.

Inside, the spacious living areas include ensuite bathrooms with freestanding baths and four-poster beds across the board. And while the one-bedroom Pool Villas are ideal for honeymoon couples seeking solitude and no distractions, the larger two-bedroom alternatives are perfect for families and small groups.

10 VILLAS À LA CARTE BREAKFAST PRIVATE VILLA POOLS RESTAURANT SPA

DWARAKA THE ROYAL VILLAS, SRI WEDARI STREET NO. 11B, UBUD, BALI, INDONESIA
+62 361 4792599 | INFO@DWARAKAVILLAS.COM | WWW.DWARAKAVILLAS.COM

BOUTIQUE
HOTEL   78   SOUTH-EAST ASIA
SELECTION

Further up the scale, the President Suite is an object lesson in how the privileged classes live; facing the rice fields this two-storey, four-bedroom villa boasts two living-rooms, a private Jacuzzi and swimming pool and a large garden.

However, there is no finer example of the ultimate accommodation than the Puri Taman Sukawati, a spectacularly detailed replica of a Balinese royal house. Helped by the fact that Dwaraka resort is owned by a member of Bali's own royal family, this three-bedroom mini-palace combines the luxury, amenities and atmosphere of a penthouse suite with the extravagance and grounds of a typical royal residence. Essentially a window to a regal world, it is as spellbinding and compelling as a childhood daydream.

That said, despite such decadence,

if the temptation to relax is trumped by an unassailable urge to explore, there is plenty to see and experience within just a few kilometres of the compound. From sessions with a yoga master to traditional Balinese dance lessons or exploratory rides on the complimentary bikes, the lengthy list of local pursuits includes one particular activity that deserves its own recommendation: an excursion to the nearby Monkey Forest, home to thousands of long-tailed macaques. Living high up in the trees surrounding the ancient Hindu temples, these mischievous simians are known for entertaining and bewildering visitors with their tourist-savvy bravura and flagrant food theft. Vigilance is advised if snacks and picnic lunches are to be retained exclusively for human consumption.

Of course, a holiday in Bali would

not be complete without at least a starter course in Indonesian cooking, and Dwaraka is well-equipped to provide lessons at all levels. A visit to the local morning market yields the compulsory fresh ingredients, before the resort's chefs dispense their expertise in different techniques and styles. And for guests who prefer to be catered for, the kitchen team will prepare a range of healthy, organic dishes influenced by recipes and signature dishes from around the world. It is all very international and yet so very Balinese.

So, if the dream of a royal hideaway rich in colour, culture and peace is as appealing as it sounds, try a few days at Dwaraka the Royal Villas and live the reverie for real. **BHS**

KAYUMANIS JIMBARAN PRIVATE ESTATE AND SPA

Bali, Indonesia

Prioritizing comfort, romance and personal service, this idyllic honeymoon destination is hidden away between a tropical garden and the coconut trees of Jimbaran Bay.

20 VILLAS · 24-HOUR BUTLER SERVICE · BAR · BEACH · CHILD-FRIENDLY · RESTAURANT · WEDDINGS

KAYUMANIS JIMBARAN PRIVATE ESTATE AND SPA, JL. YOGA PERKANTHI, JIMBARAN, KUTA SEL.,
KABUPATEN BADUNG, BALI 80364, INDONESIA
+ 62 361 705 777 | EXPERIENCE@KAYUMANIS.COM | WWW.KAYUMANIS.COM

BOUTIQUE HOTEL SELECTION · 80 · SOUTH-EAST ASIA

Part of a sprawling Balinese estate on the island's southern coast, these traditionally built one- and two-bedroom villas were originally conceived for long-stay guests. However, in the last few years, Kayumanis Jimbaran has morphed into a short-stay holiday destination in its own right. Located next to an ancient fishing settlement and near a lively marketplace, the village's pristine beachfront provides a tidy metaphor for the immaculate grounds and villas within the resort.

Open, spacious and with a notable emphasis on the cultivation and celebration of love and romance, each property benefits from a private swimming pool and timber terrace. Boasting either a king-size canopied bed or Hollywood twins in addition to a spa-like open-air bathroom, each villa is also fitted with a fully equipped kitchen.

Despite this, the authentic Indonesian cuisine produced in the on-site Kayumanis Resto ticks all the necessary gourmet boxes on its own. From within his customized Javanese joglo, Chef Oka and the team prepare a menu of modern and classic dishes inspired by the surrounding islands, taking guests on a flavourful journey across the archipelago. Employing market-fresh ingredients to create signature dishes including traditional Balinese smoked duck and mind-bendingly delicious desserts such as Es Goreng – fried ice-cream served with a white berry sauce – his creations are as confounding as they are ground-breaking.

The award-winning Kayumanis Spa, meanwhile, combines the dual power of aromatherapy oils with the skilled hands of its therapists. Offering a range of treatments either in the dedicated rooms or in the privacy of one's own villa, the expert team leads guests on a remarkable journey aimed at abandoning exhaustion and stress and replacing it with vitality, energy and refreshment.

Thankfully, unlike an increasing number of luxury destinations these days, Kayumanis Jimbaran Private Estates and Spa is purposefully equipped to welcome and entertain younger visitors as well as parents.

With vast open, green areas, shady palms and the gentle waters of Jimbaran Bay nearby, the resort is perfectly suited to hosting families as well as loved-up couples.

In fact, with its superb facilities, professional staff, stunning location and family-friendly atmosphere, everything about this glorious destination reflects the spirit of Balinese life. BHS

KAYUMANIS UBUD PRIVATE VILLA AND SPA

Bali, Indonesia

A romantic hideaway in the heart of Bali's legendary Ubud, this charming collection of villas is concealed amid a tropical forest of cinnamon trees next to the Ayung River.

Taking the indoor–outdoor experience to an unprecedented new level, these thatched-roof villas represent the peak of Balinese luxury and discretion. Situated a few kilometres from the hallowed Ubud Palace and linked by a labyrinth of interconnecting jungle paths, the expansive setting belies the fact there are 23 separate properties sharing the same space.

Set in 2.5 hectares, each of the one-, two- and three-bedroom cottages features a private pool, kitchenette and open-air bathroom. Assisted, if required, by an on-call personal butler, guests may pick from a selection of activities including yoga, trekking, cycling tours and Balinese cookery lessons. The latter involves visiting a traditional local market accompanied by a Kayumanis chef to select the key ingredients for preparation in the villa later that evening. As a window onto the world of daily life, culture and traditions here, the experience guarantees to broaden the imagination and enrich one's own repertoire back home.

A further resort highlight, the Kayumanis Spa plays host to a wide range of therapies and treatments. Housed in a traditional-style building constructed from indigenous materials including hardwood and local thatch, the spa is designed to accommodate just one couple at a time. From head and body massages and natural yoghurt scrubs to facials, shiatsu, acupressure and other ancient rejuvenating techniques, everything here aims to restore vitality and stimulate the soul. However, the key difference between Kayumanis and just about every other comparable facility lies in its flexibility; not only is there a varied selection of beauty and healing treatments within the spa itself, they may also be performed in the guest's own villa. This indoor–outdoor experience consequently makes available the skills and hands of the therapists in whichever environment the guest feels most comfortable.

23 POOL VILLAS · 24-HOUR BUTLER SERVICE · COMPLIMENTARY DAILY SHUTTLES TO UBUD TOWN

INFINITY POOL · NO CHILDREN UNDER 16 · RESTAURANT · SPA · WEDDINGS · YOGA

KAYUMANIS UBUD PRIVATE VILLA AND SPA, JL. RAYA SAYAN BR. BAUNG, UBUD, BALI 80571, INDONESIA
+62 361 972 777 | EXPERIENCE@KAYUMANIS.COM | WWW.KAYUMANIS.COM

BOUTIQUE HOTEL SELECTION · 82 · SOUTH-EAST ASIA

Similarly, the resort's restaurant serves a blend of classic Thai and contemporary Western cuisine. Perched high over a river valley, Dining Corner is open all day and serves extravagant Thai lunches, afternoon teas, romantic candlelit dinners and even caters for barbeque parties. The background soundtrack of waterfalls and cicadas does much to enhance the overall jungle-garden setting, although as with the spa treatments, all meals are transferrable from restaurant to villas if preferred.

Likewise, the Wine Corner concept is aimed at connoisseurs and is designed to showcase a collection of fine Balinese wines, produced in what are probably the closest vineyards to the equator on the planet.

An exemplar of Balinese hospitality, the service at Kayumanis Ubud is always attentive without being intrusive, and the staff bring to proceedings a rare but refreshing combination of professionalism and informality. Indeed, so committed is the company

to the development of local talent and skills that the staff here consider themselves part of the Kayumanis 'family' and in turn reward the resort with unconditional loyalty.

Ideal for honeymoons, weddings, anniversaries or simply a romantic getaway break, this dreamy retreat is arguably one of the finest destinations in Indonesia. Comprising glorious accommodation, award-winning spa facilities, fine dining and exemplary service, it is also among the most irresistible. BHS

THE UBUD VILLAGE RESORT AND SPA

Bali, Indonesia

Set in six hectares of verdant Balinese hillside, this sprawling collection of thatched-roof villas is a credit to the imagination and foresight of one man and his wife.

30 VILLAS BAR COFFEE SHOP INFINITY POOL RESTAURANT SPA

THE UBUD VILLAGE RESORT AND SPA, JALAN RAYA NYUH KUNING, PENGOSEKAN, UBUD, BALI 80571, INDONESIA
+62 361 978444 | RESERVATION@THEUBUDVILLAGE.COM | WWW.THEUBUDVILLAGE.COM

BOUTIQUE HOTEL SELECTION · 84 · SOUTH-EAST ASIA

Popular among couples, newlyweds and families alike, each of the 30 Balinese-style villas benefits from a private pool, air conditioning, marble floors and rice-paddy views.

Spotting the tourism potential of Monkey Forest more than two decades ago, long before anyone else had identified its charms on a commercial scale, Agus Wiyasa Pande is a true pioneer in Balinese hospitality. His grand plan to design and build a luxury boutique resort nearby, without the removal of a single tree, was at the time judged by many locals to be too ambitious. Pressing ahead regardless, by 2006 Agus had created Ubud Village Resort and Spa, a spacious, laid-back, tree-filled retreat that has now become one of the most desirable destinations in the region. Popular among couples, newlyweds and families alike, each of the 30 Balinese-style villas benefits from a private pool, air conditioning, marble floors and rice-paddy views. Several larger villas are also available, complete with second bedroom and fully equipped kitchen.

The restaurant, meanwhile, is a two-storey testament to old-fashioned Indonesian cooking and fine dining. Set in a pavilion overlooking water features illuminated by traditional lanterns, Angkul Angkul serves Balinese and international dishes using the finest ingredients. Candlelit dinners and private barbeques within the villas themselves are available by request, and guests may also recreate favourite recipes via the in-house cookery classes.

Close by, the on-site Kama Karana two-storey spa lists an assortment of impossibly exotic beauty treatments and therapies, while the Paddy Coffee Shop's pastries and cakes provide all-day amusement of a more leisured, indulgent nature.

The scope for recreation and entertainment at Ubud Village is both wide and rewarding, with activities including Balinese dance lessons, outdoor yoga, elephant-riding and white-water rafting. However, for the ultimate distraction, nothing beats Monkey Forest. Home to a tribe of long-tailed macaques, this dense, lush habitat is an exceptional environment in which to observe and interact with these entertaining little critters.

Full of mischief and clearly aware of their brazen charisma, they think little of swooping down and relieving unsuspecting tourists of snacks and picnic lunches. It's like they see it as a right, and their chutzpah makes a visit to this alternative Enchanting Forest all the more engaging.

Indeed, it is this light-hearted-but-luxurious, quirky-but-comfortable approach that makes Ubud Village Resort and Spa so appealing. Built on the Balinese principle of 'Tri Hita Karana' – harmony with nature, the Gods and the people – it represents the very best of Balinese hospitality. As a sustainable tourism business, it ranks among the very best of sustainable Balinese tourism and hospitality. BHS

HANSAR BANGKOK

Bangkok, Thailand

The first of four hotels (q.v.) created by Thai entrepreneur Boon Chayavichitsilp, Hansar Bangkok is the archetypal urban retreat. Relatively secluded yet only minutes away from a labyrinth of bars and restaurants, it provides a welcome break for weary tourists. With its beautifully proportioned, lavishly equipped rooms, this flagship hotel set the tone for what is now one of Thailand's fastest-growing hospitality operators.

Situated on Ratchadamri Road, in the middle of the city's most prestigious shopping district, Hansar's leaf-clad tower stands tall and distinctive among the Giant's Jungle of downtown Bangkok. This is just as well; alighting from the Skytrain into 100% humidity and walking the short distance into the air-conditioned sanctuary of the hotel lobby is a profoundly visceral experience. For the uninitiated it is akin to jumping

Tucked away on a side road in the heart of Bangkok, Hansar's debut property acts as a merciful refuge from the genial madness of one of the world's greatest cities.

94 SUITES FIVE SUITE TYPES BAR FINE DINING RESTAURANT FITNESS CENTRE POOL SPA

HANSAR BANGKOK, 3/250 SOI MAHADLEKLUANG, 2 RAJDAMRI ROAD, BANGKOK, THAILAND
+66 2 209 1234 | INFO@HANSARHOTELS.COM | WWW.HANSARBANGKOK.COM

BOUTIQUE HOTEL SELECTION 88 SOUTH-EAST ASIA

Famed for their friendliness and generosity of spirit, Thai people – and Hansar staff in particular – are joyful, discreet and always willing to help.

into a plunge pool on the hottest day of summer, or removing one's ski boots after an extended day on the slopes.

Equally worthy of note is the greeting on arrival. Famed for their friendliness and generosity of spirit, Thai people – and Hansar staff in particular – are joyful, discreet and always willing to help.

The 94 rooms include five levels of suite, all of which can accommodate up to three guests. Combining homelike amenities with intuitively designed workspaces, the Studio suite is ideal for both business and leisure travellers, while the Urban – considered Hansar Bangkok's signature room – is equipped with separate living-room and a unique interior garden.

The Edge suites, on the other hand, are designed with silk panelling, room partitions, a vertical interior garden and cantilever daybed. Similarly, Vertigo is a generously proportioned mini-apartment that includes a cantilever bedroom, walk-in bathroom and plenty of space in which to work and relax. However, at 125 square metres, the Loft is the largest suite at Hansar Bangkok. Arranged over two storeys with separate living-room and additional restroom, it is ideal for business meetings, private dinners and even movie screenings.

In common with all Hansar properties, food takes centre stage. From champagne and oysters in the Rouge Bar and traditional Japanese sushi and stew in the Arizuki Restaurant, an exemplary meal is only ever a forkful away. And for those seeking true fine dining, Eve Restaurant offers exquisite French-Mediterranean cuisine and an exclusive-use room for special occasions.

If ultimate fulfilment is key, the hotel's signature Luxsa Spa and outdoor saltwater infinity pool are ethereal in their capacity to relax and de-stress. Employing traditional Thai medicines and a range of healing and massage techniques, it is arguably the most revitalizing, rewarding health club around.

Ultimately, that sums up the ethos of Hansar Bangkok. In this restless, wonderfully addictive city of the senses, the presence of such a quiet, peaceful retreat can entirely transform the visitor experience. Simply put, when eyes have seen it all and legs begin to buckle, this hotel provides the ultimate bolthole in which to clear the mind and liberate cramping muscles. It is an indulgent island in a restless sea of chaos, conviviality and culture, and it represents the difference between merely enjoying Bangkok and falling in love with it completely. **BHS**

PURIPUNN BABY GRAND BOUTIQUE HOTEL

Chiang Mai, Thailand

Located in the heart of the ancient Lanna Thai kingdom, of which Chiang Mai is the capital, Puripunn is a Lanna Colonial-style establishment with a difference. Designed to emulate a home-from-home experience and situated just one kilometre from the main rail station, the hotel shelters guests from the tourist crowds in Thailand's northern capital.

Once an important stopover for routes between the ancient Chinese Empire and the coast of Burma, Chiang Mai achieves an important double feat: although it is steeped in history and is consequently one of the country's most popular urban destinations, these days it is largely residential. Indeed, a sprawling metropolis has sprouted up around ancient Chiang Mai, ringed by twisted vines of access routes and superhighways. Modern Thai houses and traveller hotels now lie alongside period monasteries, making it feel more like a country retreat than a busy capital city. After the benevolent chaos of Bangkok it comes as something of a welcome relief.

Generous in size with high ceilings, wood floors and a Jacuzzi bath, Puripunn's air-conditioned Superior Rooms are equipped with both private veranda and daybed, and two pairs of rooms may be interconnected.

Ground-level Deluxe Rooms, on the other hand, feature ensuite bathroom with specially designed bathtub and separate rain shower. Ideal for guests with mobility issues, these are also conveniently accessible for garden walks and the swimming pool.

The Family Room is large enough for those travelling with children, while the Baby Suites are single-bedroom affairs

A charming boutique hotel combining traditional Thai architecture with character, attentive service and modern amenities.

30 ROOMS GYM POOL RESTAURANT SPA

PURIPUNN BABY GRAND BOUTIQUE HOTEL, 104/1, CHAROEN MUEANG SOI 2, CHAOREN MUEANG ROAD, T. WAT GATE, A. MUANG, CHIANG MAI 50000, THAILAND
+66 53 302 898 | INFO@PURIPUNN.COM | WWW.PURIPUNN.COM

BOUTIQUE HOTEL SELECTION 90 SOUTH-EAST ASIA

Designed to emulate a home-from-home experience and situated just one kilometre from the main rail station, the hotel shelters guests from the tourist crowds in Thailand's northern capital.

with either en suite Jacuzzi or vintage bath. Finally, as Puripunn's signature room, the sizeable olive-green Grand Suite comes with private pool, separate living areas, twin wash-hand basins, Jacuzzi and separate rain shower.

Should the need arise, the spa facility offers specialist Thai massages, while the hotel restaurant prepares breakfast, lunch, dinner and a particularly remarkable Thai-style high tea. Serving a range of local specialities on authentic English Bone china crockery, the latter presents a gloriously satisfying cultural quirk as well as an interesting dichotomy between traditional and 'colonial' Chiang Mai: contrary to popular opinion, Thailand was the only South-East Asian state to avoid European rule in the 19th and early 20th centuries, and yet so many supposedly British influences 'remain' in the country to this day. It is an engaging if somewhat baffling oddity, and yet it makes the Puripunn Baby Grand even more unorthodox, intriguing and tempting. BHS

HANSAR KHAO YAI

Khao Yai, Thailand

Newly opened at the entrance to Thailand's most popular national park, this remote rural getaway was conceived to help isolate and dilute the stresses of everyday life.

Fulfilling a crucial dual role in its quest to attract weary but inquisitive travellers, Hansar's latest venture also seeks to appeal to those in search of excitement. In common with its sister establishments (q.v.), Khao Yai was founded on the principles of refinement, relaxation and world-class refreshment; where it differs is in the execution of this company-wide commitment. In welcoming guests to its tropical wilderness, the hotel is implicitly seeking permission to introduce them to a delightfully different way of life.

One look at the website confirms its intentions: in place of the customary shots of beaches, cocktails and deckchairs, there is an aerial view of a lush, feral, jungle-like environment. Dominated by a bright-white, three-storey modernist complex set against a backdrop of dense forest and steep-sided peaks, it is an arresting sight.

Inside, there are familiar Hansar touches, including teakwood floors and furniture, spacious living areas and spectacular views through the full-length windows. However, there also exists a fine balance between rest and recreation. For while the presence of the signature Luxsa Spa signifies a determination to cosset and revitalize, the real emphasis is on rejuvenation through exercise, exploration and self-discovery. There are no saltwater infinity pools here . . .

As a UNESCO World Heritage Site and the third-largest national park in Thailand, Khao Yai plays host to more than 3,000 plant species and a similar spread of birds, in addition to at least 60 species of mammal. From the Asian black bear and

35 ROOMS   THREE ROOM TYPES   FITNESS CENTRE
INDOOR AND OUTDOOR ACTIVITIES   LUXSA SPA   POOL   RESTAURANT

HANSAR KHAO YAI, 223 MOO 10, TAMBON MU SI, NAKHON RATCHASIMA 30130, THAILAND
+66 2209 1234 | INFO@HANSARHOTELS.COM | WWW.HANSARHOTELS.COM

As a UNESCO World Heritage Site and the third-largest national park in Thailand, Khao Yai plays host to more than 3,000 plant species and a similar spread of birds, in addition to at least 60 species of mammal.

Asian elephant, to the gaur, the gibbon and the pig-tailed macaque, it is one of the most biodiverse areas in the country.

Consequently, hotel guests are able to draw from an exhaustive list of wildlife-related activities, including night-time safaris and nature hikes. Add boxing lessons, Thai massages, kayaking excursions and dawn yoga classes, and it soon becomes clear that kicking back with a book is perhaps better suited to bedtime.

Meanwhile, as with all Hansar hotels, the food here is an object lesson in refinement. Led by Charles, the resort's de facto project manager and all-round visionary, Khao Yai's chefs serve typical country fare with a conspicuous but welcome contemporary twist. From lavish, organic salad lunches to freshly prepared al fresco barbeque dinners, the emphasis is focused on the preparation of authentic dishes that are untainted by Western influences and pseudo-fusions. Sourcing produce from the hotel's own organic vegetable garden, the chefs clearly prioritize simplicity and subtlety over extravagance and indulgence. Essentially, it is exquisite Thai food without the attendant guilt.

Only two hours from the capital and blessed with a breathtaking if somewhat sobering location, Khao Yai's fresh new rural escape has effectively created a class of its own. With its unique identity, liberal philosophy, extraordinary spa treatments and untamed surroundings, it fuses fitness and relaxation into one irresistible package. **BHS**

HANSAR PRANBURI RESORT

Khiri Khan, Thailand

Hidden among the mountains of Sam Roi Yot National Park and overlooking the Gulf of Thailand, this beguiling resort is as close as it gets to the dictionary definition of paradise.

17 ROOMS · BAR · BEACH · PET-FRIENDLY · POOL · RESTAURANT

HANSAR PRANBURI RESORT, 223–224 MOO 5, SAM ROI YOT, PRACHUAKHIRIKHAN 77120, THAILAND
+66 2209 1234 | INFO@HANSARHOTELS.COM | WWW.HANSARPRANBURI.COM

BOUTIQUE
HOTEL
SELECTION
94
SOUTH-EAST ASIA

Pranburi offers an engaging assortment of excursions and adventures in the surrounding area. From hiking in the Phraya Nakhon Cave to pleasure-cruising around secluded bays and coves aided by a private-beach butler, there is always an activity on the go.

It is fair to assume that many people's view of paradise, in their mind's eye at least, probably includes a lengthy stretch of beach with white sands, waving palm trees and turquoise waters – perhaps with a tropical island on the horizon and a pair of sun-loungers or deckchairs in the foreground. If this sounds familiar to the point of cliché, that is perfectly reasonable. However, it also accurately reflects the philosophy of Pranburi Resort.

The former holiday home of a British expat, this private residential retreat forms part of Thai hotelier Boon Chayavichitsilp's burgeoning portfolio of Hansar-branded hotels. Combining deftly executed design and detail with the world-famous warmth of Thai people, the group is changing the face of hospitality in Thailand, in part due to the success of this outstanding island escape. Set against a backdrop of vividly coloured Bougainvillea plants, Pranburi is uncannily Mediterranean-like in its appearance. With a total of 17 rooms split between the main villa and independent bungalows, the resort invites guests to tailor-make their own experiences, explore the surrounding coves and bays and even choose accommodation based on the vistas.

Of these, the Garden View rooms were designed with luxury and privacy as the priorities. Nestled between the 300 peaks of the Sam Roi Yot National Park, these liberating spaces benefit from ceiling-high windows leading out onto wood-panelled terraces. Meanwhile, with its private Jacuzzi and beach-view balcony, the enchanting Honeymoon Suite implores couples to shed their inhibitions and celebrate their love.

For a different outlook altogether, the resort's Sea View rooms prioritize spellbinding ocean vistas. Just imagine sitting out on the balcony sharing breakfast together and watching the sun rise over the water; it doesn't get more picture-postcard.

And for guests who feel the need to explore, Pranburi offers an engaging assortment of excursions and adventures in the surrounding area. From hiking in the Phraya Nakhon Cave to pleasure-cruising around secluded bays and coves aided by a private-beach butler, there is always an activity on the go. Alternatively, staying put in the resort comes with its own specific benefits, including a saltwater infinity pool and the availability of in-room massages. And when hunger itself eventually surfaces, the hotel's brigade of world-class chefs will demonstrate their considerable skills in the open-plan kitchen.

For anyone struggling to picture in their mind's eye their childhood vision of the mythical Promised Land, a break at this luxury beachside hideaway will sufficiently refresh and intensify the memory. BHS

ZEAVOLA RESORT

Koh Phi Phi, Thailand

With its jungle-garden setting, paradisiacal beach and PADI-accredited diving centre, Zeavola Resort represents a passport to rejuvenation and underwater exploration.

53 VILLAS AIRPORT TRANSFER BAR BEACH CARDIO ROOM POOL RESTAURANT SPA WEDDINGS

ZEAVOLA RESORT, 11 MOO 8 LAEM TONG, KOH PHI PHI, AO NANG, KRABI 81000, THAILAND
+66 7562 7000 | RESERVATION@ZEAVOLA.COM | WWW.ZEAVOLA.COM

BOUTIQUE
HOTEL   96   SOUTH-EAST ASIA
SELECTION

Set on Koh Phi Phi's Laem Tong beach, these romantic detached villas are notably reminiscent of a bygone age and are as close as one gets to the definition of barefooted freedom. Connected by a labyrinth of pathways, this beautiful Thai village sits amid dense tropical foliage and greenery, with several of the cottages situated just metres from the shore. While these provide the requisite beachfront setting, the remaining villas, set deeper into the forest, are more sheltered.

With a choice of four styles of suite, each offering its own signature facilities and attractions, this sporadic collection is spread out among the lush green rainforest. Split across two levels and blessed with 180-degree views of the sapphire-blue Andaman Sea, the spacious Pool Villas were designed with honeymooners and hopeless romantics in mind. Equipped with private swimming pool and outdoor showers, these luxury chalets encourage couples to elope to the hills for romantic escapes with no interruptions.

Down by the shore, the three exclusively positioned Beachfront Suites invite the most fortunate guests directly onto the white sands at the edge of the resort. Featuring an expansive outdoor living area and stunning ocean vistas, these 60-square-metre residences even benefit from full-length windows to help circulate the essential sea breeze. Meanwhile, scattered around huge tropical trees, the Garden Suites combine large outdoor living spaces with king-size bed, air conditioning, full-length windows and multimedia entertainment. Guests may also choose between interior or exterior showers, while bamboo blinds shield somnolent eyes from the world outside. Finally, it is a short jaunt along the sandy pathways to the smaller Village Suites. With separate dressing area and outdoor living-room, the 11 immaculately presented chalets inspire both relaxation and celebration, complementing the eco-resort's reputation as a popular wedding venue. Indeed, Zeavola has hosted over 80 Buddhist and Western-style ceremonies over the last few years, with guests taking advantage of the exceptional setting and pristine beach. And, never more than a short wander away from any of the villas, the spa supplies a range of therapies of which Phi Phi Lomi – a combination of Polynesian Lomi Lomi and Thai Massage – is the signature treatment.

With island boat trips, snorkelling excursions and diving at the five-star PADI-accredited on-site dive centre, Zeavola is a romantic hideaway that opens a clear-blue underwater door to Thailand's mesmerizing submarine world. BHS

HANSAR SAMUI

Koh Samui, Thailand

Situated just yards from a pristine stretch of white sand overlooking Bophut Bay in the Gulf of Thailand, this enchanting hotel sits blissfully in a class of its own.

74 ROOMS AWARD-WINNING SPA BAR FITNESS CENTRE

GOURMET RESTAURANT INFINITY POOL PRIVATE BEACHFRONT

HANSAR SAMUI, 101/28 MOO 1, BOPHUT KOH SAMUI, SURAT THANI 84320, THAILAND
+66 77 245511 | RESERVATION@HANSARSAMUI.COM | WWW.HANSARSAMUI.COM

BOUTIQUE
HOTEL   98   SOUTH-EAST ASIA
SELECTION

Built in 2010 in a traditional Thai fishing village, Hansar Samui takes the freedom and peace of beachfront living to an extraordinary new level. Constructed largely from local textiles and materials, each of the hotel's suites features an outdoor living area and a bewilderingly comfortable bed.

With walk-in rain shower, teak flooring, full-length French windows and sheltered balcony, the Sea View rooms evoke a rare degree of solitude. Further up the scale, with open-plan bathrooms large and luxurious enough to rival the bedrooms, the Sea View XL accommodation adds a four-poster bed and 50 per cent more living space. And for the ultimate in luxury and grandeur, the exclusive Beach Front suites are hard to beat. Blending outstanding facilities with awe-inspiring seascapes, these rooms represent the zenith of this legendary paradise.

Meanwhile, a soak in the freestanding bathtub available in both the XL and Beach Front accommodation highlights a uniquely satisfying paradox: on the one hand, the vistas may be enjoyed with absolute privacy from the comfort of a rose-filled tub of steaming hot water; on the other, the sea view opens a window onto the daily privileges of a typical beach lifeguard. The overall feeling is akin to actually being in a bath, on a beach, with no one else around. It is, quite simply, phenomenal.

Fortunately, mornings here are the same for everyone. Blinking in the light of a Koh Samui sunrise, a dive into the ocean-facing infinity pool swiftly erases any trace of languor before a visit to the resort's award-winning Luxsa Spa.

Specializing in a range of local treatments practised by highly experienced therapists, the facility affords the opportunity to comprehensively unwind before the day even begins. From soothing aromatherapy remedies to traditional Thai massages, body wraps and facials, Luxsa is a rejuvenation station for muscles and mind.

Emerging into the sunshine, all that is immediately required is a decision on what to do next. Given the location, it is worth beginning this process with a contemplative rest in a deckchair, observing in the process the genial waiting staff apparently walking on water to serve refreshments on the far side of the pool.

Eventually, as hunger gradually wins its war, the exhaustive list of apéritifs and pre-dinner cocktails of the laid-back H Bistro Restaurant will inevitably start to beckon. Specializing in Thai-style fine dining under the culinary stewardship of executive chef Stephen Jean Dion, the kitchen team prepare multi-course menus by fusing together the four senses of sight, scent, texture and taste. With everything from fresh Maine lobster to Canadian oysters, complemented by a handpicked list of international wines and champagnes, the French-Mediterranean menu is pretty close to culinary perfection.

With its astonishing seascapes, simple architecture, modern facilities and traditional spa this beachside escape provides a remarkable sanctuary in which to take refuge from the tension and tedium of life back home. **BHS**

VILLA KALYANA

Koh Samui, Thailand

Enjoy a family-friendly break in this exclusive-use estate with infinity pool, private stretch of Samui South Beach and accommodation for over 30 guests.

`20 ROOMS` ADJOINING ROOMS AVAILABLE AIR CONDITIONING BAR CINEMA ROOM FAMILY-FRIENDLY
GYM INFINITY POOL PRIVATE BAY AND BEACHFRONT ROOFTOP TERRACE SPA

VILLA KALYANA, 113/5 LAEM SOR BEACH, SANTI SOOK 1 ROAD, TALING NGAM, KOH SAMUI, SURAT THANI 84140, THAILAND
+44 208 672 7040 | INFO@MYPRIVATEVILLAS.COM | WWW.VILLAKALYANASAMUI.COM

BOUTIQUE HOTEL SELECTION 100 SOUTH-EAST ASIA

Holidays with children in tow are curious affairs. On the one hand, parents may be keen to stay close to their kids and share the relaxation, laughter and joy of a familial getaway; on the other, such adventures can be exhausting for all concerned, with adults often desperate to shut themselves away from the bickering, the temper tantrums and the sibling rivalry. While this represents something approaching the norm for families of all backgrounds, size and culture, it can make for an arduous atmosphere in advance of and during the vacation itself. Indeed, the process of locating a suitable property may be as fraught with tension and frustration as the inevitable last-minute dash to the airport to catch the flight.

Fortunately, Koh Samui's Villa Kalyana is equipped to handle such routine challenges. Situated in a prime location overlooking Laem Sor Bay, the stunning mini-village accommodates up to 36 adults and several children in its 20 bedrooms. Spread between the main pavilion and eight beach-bungalow suites, this tropical seafront residence and private beachfront is ideal for holidays, get-togethers, celebrations and parties. Dispersed across expansive tropical gardens and palm tree plantations, the bungalows are arranged around an exclusive-use swimming pool, with space in the surrounding area to host more than 100 party guests. Elsewhere, the main villa itself features individually styled bedrooms furnished with four-poster king-size beds and large outdoor terraces, while the nearby movie room and games area will keep the kids entertained for days on end.

Outside, the 300-square-metre infinity pool with dual islands and children's play area is flanked by outdoor lounge areas and a large covered terrace. And with snorkelling trips, jet-skiing excursions, complimentary sea kayaks and even powerboat hire just along the beach, the chances of finding little to do are simply non-existent.

Later, when hunger raises its head – as it frequently does with children around – dining here presents options for everyone. From a candlelit beach dinner under the stars to the air-conditioned dining-room's 24-seater banqueting table and the in-villa dishes prepared by the resort's own private chef, all tastes are catered for at Villa Kalyana.

Indeed, so flawless is the combined package of location, layout and facilities, it is uncannily reminiscent of a private island. With ample space, luxurious accommodation and an army of staff helping the adults to outnumber children by at least two to one, the resort provides the ideal ratio for a relaxing break on tropical shores. It is, essentially, the ultimate family playground. BHS

VILLA MOONSHADOW

Koh Samui, Thailand

Located in a genuinely jaw-dropping spot overlooking the Gulf of Thailand, this recently completed phenomenon sets a new standard in rural exclusive-use villas.

4 ROOMS   INFINITY POOL   OCEAN VIEWS   PRIVATE AIR-CONDITIONED SUV CHAUFFEUR SERVICE FOR HIRE
SUNDECK AND PRIVATE TERRACES   TROPICAL GARDENS   YOGA, THAI MASSAGE AND COOKING LESSONS

VILLA MOONSHADOW, 104/57 BOPHUT, KO SAMUI 84320, THAILAND
+66 077 423 495 | INFO@VILLA-MOONSHADOW.COM | WWW.VILLA-MOONSHADOW.COM

A deep intake of breath followed by a barely audible gulp; there is simply no other realistic reaction when accessing Villa Moonshadow's website for the first time. Rotating on a 30-second loop, the four panoramic homepage photographs explain more in half a minute than any guidebook, testimonial or review could elucidate in 20 pages.

Constructed in 2013 on the summit of Chaweng Noi Hill, this extraordinarily attractive villa is close enough for easy access to the lively town below it, yet sufficiently isolated to guarantee absolute privacy. A triumph of contemporary architectural design, the three armadillo-shaped pavilions sit in a prime location, high above the bay. With the principal, tech-heavy accommodation and living area in front, the two smaller independent structures sit behind, each housing two ensuite bedrooms. Ocean views are visible throughout, courtesy of glass walls and doors, floor-to-ceiling windows and plenty of height and space inside. A sea breeze cools the interior, highlighting a deliberate eco-friendly design detail: one of several such innovations, the system naturally cools the villa through a waterfall power system, neutralizing the need for air conditioning in the main social space.

Outside is even more attractive, with tropical gardens, sun-loungers, an open dining area and relaxation pods adorning the deck. However, few would argue that Villa Moonshadow's defining characteristic is the boat-shaped infinity pool stretching out over the side of the cliff. Flowing imperceptibly into the

horizon beyond, its height and position above the bay lends the impression of both vertiginous dominance and, curiously, an oceanic ha-ha.

As Moonshadow's centrepiece, this agonizingly pretty swimming pool is as much a part of the inside of the villa as it is the grounds; from the sunroom at the front of the main suite, the sea appears to begin where the living-room ends. Consequently, the view is as unruffled as a millpond, whatever the prevailing weather conditions.

Happily, the villa's rental price includes two members of full-time, five-star staff, both of whom live in a separate maids' house on-site. Providing housekeeping, food-storage and shopping facilities and delicious Thai cooking, they are professional yet friendly, and crucially available 24/7. Additionally, a multilingual guest manager is also on hand to organize island excursions, diving, snorkelling, fishing and boating trips, as well as to recommend the best beach clubs and restaurants. Although, with a choice of Continental, English, American, Indian, Chinese or Thai breakfasts included in

the villa rental price, it is unclear when additional nourishment will be required during the day . . .

Naturally, should the temptation ever arise to explore farther than the villa grounds, there is plenty to keep oneself occupied. As the most popular resort town and with the longest beach in Koh Samui, nearby Chaweng has much to offer in terms of sports, culture and leisure activities. Boasting natural pools, waterfalls, a marine park and jungles replete with tropical fruits, it is an engaging destination that could, if permitted, distract from Villa Moonshadow.

Fortunately, the island's most entrancing holiday home relies on its own unique qualities to capture and retain its occupants' attention. For proof, just wait until the real thing heaves into view. With its clifftop position, infinite seascapes, luxury-minimalist interior and spectacular surroundings, the only thing missing is a microlight from which to fully appreciate the aerial view. But, then again, that is what the website is for. Just be sure to draw breath before hitting 'Enter'. **BHS**

VILLA CAEMILLA BOUTIQUE HOTEL

Boracay, Philippines

Situated yards from the famous white sands of Boracay, this heavenly beachside escape attracts couples, families and lone travellers in search of an isolated island getaway.

39 ROOMS BEACH KITE-SURFING RESTAURANT WATER SPORTS

VILLA CAEMILLA BOUTIQUE HOTEL, WHITE BEACH PATH, MALAY, AKLAN, PHILIPPINES
+63 917 526 9449 | RESERVATIONS@VILLACAEMILLA.COM | WWW.VILLACAEMILLA.COM

BOUTIQUE HOTEL SELECTION | 106 | SOUTH-EAST ASIA

On the face of it, no holiday location is universally attractive to the entire spectrum of tourists, particularly if it is hampered by limited transport links. Indeed, remote holidays in hard-to-reach areas are, on the whole, somewhat niche at the best of times. Consequently, such destinations attract a specific type of individual or group; those who prefer unconventional alternatives to roads and runways in order to reach them. Boracay, a small island in the Western Visayas archipelago of the Philippines, is just such a place. Accessible neither by car nor train and well-known for its tropical beaches and clear waters, in 2012 the island won 'Best in the World' from a respected international travel magazine.

Landing on the quay at Boat Station 3, the quieter end of the famous White Beach, it is not hard to imagine how this happened. At a little over 10 square kilometres and with precious few crowds or queues, Boracay is, by some margin, the most pristine, unspoiled, restful island in the region. Seated on the beach itself and hidden among a fringe of palm trees and parasols, Villa Caemilla offers a largely noiseless existence for guests, save for the breaking waves of the Jintotolo Channel. The 39 air-conditioned rooms and suites provide a varying scale of size, views and amenities, albeit with common underlying themes of freedom and luxury. From the 30-square-metre Premiere Deluxe to the Family Suite at almost three times the size and with beachfront terrace, there is accommodation to suit every taste, requirement and budget.

Fortunately, though not surprisingly in a resort of this calibre, the range of outdoor activities is comfortably in line with the indoor facilities. While snorkelling and diving are available for adventures beneath the surface, there is jet-skiing, banana-boating, parasailing and wind- and kite-surfing on offer above it. Meanwhile, just a few doors down from the hotel, the Bella Isa Spa lists several treatments and therapies, including massages, facials, wraps and scrubs. The sheer breadth of choice presents a quandary in itself: pick one or two and risk omitting the unmissable, or elect them all and accidently ignore everything else the Boracay outdoors has to offer. The good news, whichever option is favoured, is that several treatments are available in the hotel rooms themselves.

For the more socially active fun-seekers, White Beach Stations 1 and 2 provide equally attractive propositions but with enhanced opportunities for shopping, dining and socializing. However, if the combination of sunshine, sand, spa, peace and luxury is too enticing to overlook, Villa Caemilla is the one to book.

Of course, the principal reason to visit a resort of this nature is simply to escape from the treadmill and tedium of everyday life back home. With so much to offer in so preposterously glorious a setting, it is a wonder – and a blessing – that more people haven't yet discovered this Filipino paragon of paradise. BHS

EL NIDO RESORTS

Pangulasian Island, Philippines

This luxurious island escape leads the way in sustainable, environmentally friendly tourism and instils a common element of fun and adventure in every activity on offer.

42 SUITES   BAR   BEACH   BUTLER SERVICE   HELICOPTER AVAILABLE   POOL
RESTAURANT   SPA   STUNNING VIEWS   WEDDINGS

EL NIDO RESORTS, PALAWAN 5313, PHILIPPINES
+63 2 902 5990 | HOLIDAY@ELNIDORESORTS.COM | WWW.ELNIDORESORTS.COM

BOUTIQUE
HOTEL   108   SOUTH-EAST ASIA
SELECTION

Known as the 'Island of the Sun' and planted right on the apex of a tropical beach, El Nido Resorts Pangulasian Island presents 42 deluxe suites designed in traditional Filipino style. Perched on stilts some 15 to 18 metres above the forest, the eight Canopy Villas set the benchmark for ocean views. Accessed by stairs* leading to an elevated boardwalk which winds through the forest, nothing comes close to matching their splendid aerial isolation and privacy.

The 24 Beach Villas and six Pool Villas, on the other hand, are predictably situated close to water. Each benefiting from 65 square metres of floor space, plus a sizeable private balcony, they face either the crystalline ocean or their own private swimming pool.

* Buggy also available for access, where required.

Located in Bacuit Bay, El Nido Resorts was conceived with the aim of maintaining the natural topography and resources of the surrounding land.

The beach itself is a stretch of white sand almost three quarters of a kilometre in length and with the dense, lush backdrop of tropical forest behind, the resort's spa offers a bespoke menu of local Filipino treatments and therapies.

First and foremost an eco-resort, El Nido Resorts was designed in harmony with the natural beauty of the island and its resident land- and sea-based creatures and coral reefs. Located in Bacuit Bay, it was conceived with the aim of maintaining the natural topography and resources of the surrounding land. Prioritizing the preservation of local trees and foliage, its construction involved minimal disturbance to wildlife habitats, and sustainable materials were utilized throughout. It all adds up to a thoroughly responsible philosophy that underpins all aspects of the resort. Having said that, there exists a certain anomaly about this fastidious attention to detail, although it is present in an entirely positive context: after the significant effort and investment required to create a world-leading eco-resort aimed at promoting the wider benefits of sustainable tourism, it is mildly ironic that many of El Nido Resorts Pangulasian's attractions and diversions actually lie beneath the surface of the sea. The water-based activities, many of them guided by local specialists and professional instructors, comprise a significant proportion of the hobbies and pastimes here. From kayaking to secret beaches and snorkelling or scuba diving with local (benign) sharks, to exploring the coral reef just 100 metres away, the options are seemingly endless. Indeed, there is so much to do in the water – most of it harmless to the immediate environs – that it is bound to mitigate the impact that tourism has on land. It is an unusual, possibly unintentional but nonetheless pleasing paradox, and it neatly sums up the ethos of this wonderfully alluring resort: offering classic Filipino luxury, friendliness and exemplary service based around solid eco-friendly principles, El Nido Resorts Pangulasian is to responsible tourism what sunshine is to summer. BHS

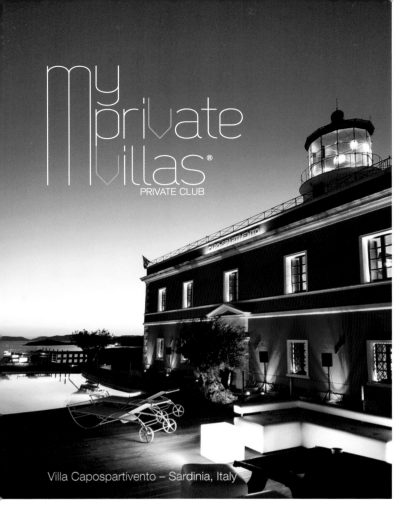

Villa Capospartivento – Sardinia, Italy

Luxury Villa Rentals Direct from Owners

A selection of the most luxurious holiday villas in the world, available to rent directly from the owners.

These amazing properties form the perfect backdrop to create unique and unforgettable experiences, whether clients are looking for a family vacation, a cultural break or organizing a special event.

My Private Villas offers discerning clients a chance to discover the most exclusive properties available for rent directly from the owners in some of the most iconic destinations around the world. Prime locations include Cote d'Azur, Amalfi Coast, Tuscany, the Balearic and Greek Islands, St Barth, Bali, South Africa, Brazil, plus the Swiss and French Alps.

Whether by the sea, in the mountains, on the lakeshore, in the city centre or nestling in vineyards or olive groves, all properties in My Private Villas collection are ideal for indulging in luxury surrounded by friends and family and having the vacation of a lifetime.

LUXURY VILLAS   LUXURY CHALETS   PRIVATE ISLANDS   LUXURY APARTMENTS

FLEXIBILITY   TRANSPARENCY   TAILOR-MADE SERVICES   24 HOURS CONCIERGE SERVICE

info@myprivatevillas.com www.myprivatevillas.com +44 (0) 208 672 7040

Villa Manresa, Mallorca, Spain

Villa Bay, Cap Ferrat, France

Private Island Tagomago, Balearic Islands, Spain

Villa Macchiavelli, Tuscany, Italy

Chalet Peak, Zermatt, Switzerland

My Private Villas collection is an eclectic mix of modern, leading edge, designer and historic houses with the portfolio offering a diverse range from private islands, beachfront properties, wine estates and city apartments to ski chalets, golf, scuba, horse riding or other sporting estates. My Private Villas team personally checks each villa regularly to ensure the standards are perfect. Whether you own an exceptional home and you want to make it available for rent or you are looking for staying in an unusual, historical or spectacular property that is not easily accessible on the market, My Private Villas will be your perfect choice.

Meet the Visionary

Passionate about travel and luxury and with a background in communication and marketing, Mr Paolo Macchiaroli, founder of the company, wanted to offer both clients and owners a different approach by creating My Private Villas.

Being in the market for 15 years and seeing it change dramatically, Paolo decided to create a private club of villa owners where transparency was the key factor along with providing a unique experience.

What distinguishes My Private Villas from any other villa rental agency is the relation the club has with the owners. Being in direct contact with them and offering them extra visibility and marketing activities, the private club receives in exchange discounts, tailor made and complimentary services which can then be provided to the clients who immediately feel that the team goes the extra mile to ensure their highest demands are met.

VIDEO ADVISOR

Video for business is no longer a luxury
but a necessity

www.videoadvisor.co.uk   info@videoadvisor.co.uk   +44 (0) 20 3011 1778

AUSTRALASIA

BHS

SAFFIRE FREYCINET

Tasmania, Australia

Soak up the eye-widening vistas, world-class service and fine Australian fare in the shadow of the Hazards Mountain Range and the mirror of Great Oyster Bay.

Across the continents there cannot be many hotel driveways nine kilometres long, but Down Under it is probably not that unusual. With half-million-hectare estates, vast swathes of the country located off the beaten track and remote homes and holiday destinations all but the norm, a bit of rough-roading is only to be expected; indeed, it is a large part of the visitor attraction to rural Australia in the first place. Nevertheless, the approach to Saffire Freycinet is, for first-time visitors, as surprising as it is authentically 'Outback'. By the time the luxury lodge materializes like a giant beached stingray, the on-arrival welcome glass of champagne looks mighty welcome indeed.

Situated in an area of East Coast Tasmania and surrounded by white-sand beaches and verdant bushland, this

20 SUITES BAR **GYM** POOL **RESTAURANT** SPA

SAFFIRE FREYCINET, 2352 COLES BAY ROAD, COLES BAY, TAS 7215, AUSTRALIA
+61 3 6256 7888 | STAY@SAFFIRE-FREYCINET.COM.AU | WWW.SAFFIRE-FREYCINET.COM.AU

futuristic but simultaneously rustic hotel comprises 20 exclusive suites. With private courtyard, outdoor decking and double shower, the Luxury variants enjoy glorious vistas and spacious, minimalist interiors. Nearby, the four Private Pavilions feature separate lounge, bedroom and dining areas, while the 10 Signature Suites are larger still and benefit from impossibly striking views. Admired through walls of glass, as opposed to mere windows, the contrasting sights of mountains, greenery and the bay below are magnified into a genuinely mesmerizing spectacle. It's like sitting front-row in a private High Definition cinema but on a bigger, even more impressive scale. And, of course, it's live.

This being Oz, however, there are plenty of local distractions vying for guests' attention. Freycinet's National Park, for example, is on the doorstep, and there is a world of deserted islands, bush and secluded beaches to explore outside the hotel. Walking, hiking, riding and mountain-biking are all encouraged, and the resultant panoramas are well worth the muscle-ache. Similarly, included in the room rates is a lengthy list of activities, from kayaking and bird-watching to vineyard tours and cooking demonstrations.

Naturally, the food here is equally outstanding, with dinner at Palate restaurant a typically Antipodean affair. The superb dégustation and à la carte menus rely heavily on indigenous produce and ingredients, showcasing full-flavoured game meats, local oysters and deep-sea fish so fresh it could have been plucked from an on-site aquarium. This

All of it – the romantic, intensely private accommodation, the boundless views and outdoor activities, the exquisite restaurant and spa – suggests why Trip Advisor recently crowned Saffire Freycinet 'Australia's Best Luxury Hotel' and 'Best Small Hotel'.

is original Australian fare as imagined by a world-class chef, and as expected it is complemented by a collection of local and national wines that pay homage to Freycinet's Mediterranean climate.

Meanwhile, for a spot of R&R, the hotel's private spa offers an exhaustive list of treatments to re-energize depleted bodies. Arguably the most impressive such facility in Australia, Spa Anise utilizes the finest indigenous skincare products as part of a series of implausibly relaxing therapies. Tailoring bespoke treatment programmes to individual requirements and preferences, the specialist staff are trained to help guests rediscover their energy and equanimity. It is difficult to overstate the spa's contribution to Saffire's reputation and indeed the guest experience as a whole.

All of this – the romantic, intensely private accommodation, the boundless views and outdoor activities, the exquisite restaurant and spa – suggests why

Trip Advisor recently crowned Saffire Freycinet 'Australia's Best Luxury Hotel' and 'Best Small Hotel'. Unsurprisingly, given the quality of its staff, it also won the 'Best Service Award'.

As a remote holiday destination that is, to all intents and purposes cut off from the world – and also reassuringly connected to the surrounding environment – this is a truly remarkable boutique retreat. That said, it is far more than the sum of its location and facilities. By way of illustration, consider the fastidious attention to detail in its provision of an exclusive lounge at the nearest main airport, Hobart International. Afforded the luxury treatment from start to finish, guests may relax and enjoy their Saffire experience right up to the moment of departure. As gestures go, it is a profoundly imaginative touch and yet another example of the qualities that ultimately make this a consummately world-class establishment. BHS

RUMOURS LUXURY VILLAS AND SPA

Rarotonga, Cook Islands

Relax and untwine in these romantic Polynesian villas, each equipped with private swimming pool and arresting views of a pristine coral lagoon.

7 VILLAS   BEACH   PERFECT FOR ROMANCE AND PRIVACY   PRIVATE POOL

PRIVATE BARBEQUE FACILITIES   SPA   TWIN BATHROOMS WITH RAIN SHOWERS

RUMOURS LUXURY VILLAS AND SPA, ARA TAPU, COOK ISLANDS
+682 22551 | INFO@RUMOURS-RAROTONGA.COM | WWW.RUMOURS-RAROTONGA.COM

BOUTIQUE HOTEL SELECTION   122   AUSTRALASIA

Step out for a wander on white sands, explore the coral reefs of the Muri Lagoon or remain within the villa grounds and take advantage of the sunshine and solitude.

Tucked away beside the turquoise waters of Rarotonga, Rumours Luxury Villas and Spa is the consummate retreat for holidaymakers, globetrotters, loved-up couples and child-free travellers. Paying homage to the traditional kikau huts of the Cook Islands, the accommodation offers sequestered privacy in walled hideaways just a few yards from the shore. Blending natural elements of traditional Polynesian architecture with modern amenities and convenience, the two-bedroom villas comprise bright, spacious living areas with high ceilings, marble flooring, Superking-size four-poster beds and blink-twice ocean views. Even the bathrooms are an experience, with skylights, dual rain showers and smoothened stones underfoot.

Emerging refreshed and ready for breakfast, it is wise to head straight for the espresso-maker. Producing a taste rivalling that of the best European cafés, this lowly machine turns users into world-class baristas at the touch of a button. Rich, flavoursome and full of body, a shot of this stuff will kick-start the day like a bucket of fresh water to the face. Rarely does home-prepared coffee taste anything like this.

Separately, a conflict of interest may also be brewing and it will become apparent shortly after breakfast. Put simply, it is the choice between stepping out for a wander on white sands and exploring the coral reefs of the Muri Lagoon, or remaining within the villa grounds and taking advantage of the sunshine and solitude. Between swimming, kayaking and snorkelling around the reef, and lounging in the spa tub or hammock tethered to the beachfront rear deck, it is a tough call.

Meanwhile, for those who have perhaps seen enough sunshine for one day, there are plenty of other distractions on offer, from taking in a movie in the Platinum Villa's private screening room to embarking on a tour of Avarua's lively Saturday market. Accessible via hire car, chauffeur-driven transport or the colourful, stop-anywhere bus service, the market comes highly recommended for those looking to sample the local way of life.

Alternatively, try joining the many islanders and tourists who congregate nightly at the end of the airport's runway to be 'jet-blasted' by incoming planes. Protected by the seawall that skirts around the approach, it is a uniquely exhilarating, life-affirming experience.

And that, essentially, is what this glorious resort is all about; it is entirely up to the individual how much they wish to participate. Scoot around on a hired moped or snooze by the pool; lounge in a deckchair, or submerge oneself in a luminescent underwater kingdom; do everything, or do nothing.

Ultimately, Rumours Luxury Villas and Spa is a world away from the rest of humanity and it is all the better for it. BHS

TAVEUNI PALMS

Taveuni Island, Fiji

*Set amid waving coconut trees on the edge of an ivory-hued beach,
this flawless tropical hideaway is perfect for weddings, honeymoons
and for relaxing in sun-soaked bliss.*

2 VILLAS   FULLY STAFFED   POOLS   PRIVATE BEACH   SPA   WATER SPORTS

TAVEUNI PALMS, P.O. BOX 51M, MATEI, TAVEUNI, FIJI
+679 888 0032 | WWW.TAVEUNIPALMS.COM | INFO@TAVEUNIPALMS.COM

On the face of it, Taveuni is as isolated as a desert island should be. Known locally as the 'Garden Island of Fiji' it is the third largest in the South Pacific archipelago and one of its best-kept secrets. Spectacularly verdant, picturesque and friendly, Taveuni Palms attracts visitors drawn to the world-class diving, bushwalks and prolific bird life in this perennially warm, welcoming destination.

Each occupying half a hectare of beachfront and served by seven members of staff who provide five-star food and service, the dual accommodation options are designed for comfort and seclusion. Sitting directly on private white sands, the air-conditioned Beach Villa boasts sweeping gardens, a private beach and swimming pool. Equipped with Superking-size beds, luxurious bathroom and an outdoor shower, it also benefits from daybed sofas, hammocks, lofted ceilings and subtle décor. Opening up along the entire frontage, its doors were designed with ocean views and sea breezes in mind.

Meanwhile, high above the Pacific Ocean sits a private, air-conditioned hut – a 'bure', in the local lexicon. But this is no ordinary hut. The centrepiece of the Horizon Spa Villa is a dizzyingly pretty infinity pool which seemingly disappears directly off the deck. It lends the impression of holidaying in a glorious stilt house, albeit without the vertigo.

With no formal restaurant at Taveuni Palms, guests are at liberty to choose their dining setting within the grounds; from private beach to villa deck, or poolside table to inside the villa itself, the setting may vary according to mood, hour or appetite. Billed as a culinary journey through the South Pacific and served by a pool of friendly staff drawn from India and the entire Pacific Rim, Fiji's rich culinary heritage is manifested on the plate through a bounty of exotic fruits,

Spectacularly verdant, picturesque and friendly, Taveuni Palms attracts visitors drawn to the world-class diving, bushwalks and prolific bird life in this perennially warm, welcoming destination.

vegetables and startlingly fresh seafood. With boundless menus and five special private dining locations, no meal is ever the same.

Revitalized and ready to explore, guests are presented with an inexhaustible catalogue of activities and distractions. From hiking and swimming to kayaking, fishing, cycling or scuba diving, there is always an energetic diversion vying for one's attention. And for those who are keen to avoid such gratuitous exertion, the resort's spa combines authentic Fijian treatments with high quality products made from the purest indigenous oils.

Taveuni Palms is, by virtue of its location, considered something of an isolated destination. But alongside the friendly staff, fresh food, sumptuous accommodation and heart-stopping views, perhaps the real beauty of the resort – and its greatest asset – is its relative accessibility. For in spite of its apparent desert-island status and perceived isolation, Taveuni is in fact just a short flight away from nearby Viti Levu, the largest and most populous island in the Republic of Fiji.

All of which means that without long and exhausting transfer journeys on arrival and departure, a break here could well end up the holiday of a lifetime. BHS

EUROPE

BHS

HOTEL HERITAGE

Bruges, Belgium

This magnificent Flemish mansion in the centre of one of Europe's most engaging cities is a monument to style, class and the highest levels of hospitality.

With a range of lovely touches including a sundeck, private sauna, steam bath and guided walking tours of the city, there is plenty to make guests feel special.

Designed in 1869 by Louis Delacenserie, a well-known native of Bruges, the building was bought and converted by Johan and Isabelle Creytens in 1992 and reopened as a hotel the following summer. As a Relais & Châteaux property, Hotel Heritage is compelled to live up to some formidable standards and expectations, and over the last two decades has garnered a stirring reputation and a clutch of global awards. Evaluated according to the France-based elite hotel's association's traditional motto of 'Caractère, Courtoisie, Calme,

22 ROOMS   BAR   BOSE SYSTEM   IN ROOM iPAD   RESTAURANT   SAUNA   STEAM BATH

HOTEL HERITAGE, NIKLAAS DESPARSSTRAAT 11, 8000 BRUGES, BELGIUM
+32 50 444 444 | MANAGER@HOTEL-HERITAGE.COM | WWW.HOTEL-HERITAGE.COM

BOUTIQUE
HOTEL   131   EUROPE
SELECTION

The in-house restaurant, Le Mystique, serves local Belgian and Flanders specialities including Duroc bacon, codfish, venison and, yes, a range of chocolate and patisserie items so delicious and guilt-inducing it could make grown men weep.

Charme et Cuisine', there are a number of strict admission standards to must adhere. Most properties are converted historic landmarks such as manor houses, townhouses and castles, and in addition to luxurious facilities and gold-standard service, associates are obliged to offer certain special features to help distinguish them from their chain-run counterparts.

Opulently appointed with intricate chandeliers, antique furniture and rich, indulgent décor, Hotel Heritage's 22 bedrooms vary in size but are largely on a par with each other for service, facilities and amenities. Equipped with Nilson queen-size or twin beds, marble bathrooms, individual temperature controls and Nespresso coffee machines, the rooms and suites are positioned to make the most of the panoramic cityscapes. With views of Bruges and many of its instantly recognizable landmarks, the Junior Suites are spacious and exceptional in their attention to

detail. And with a range of special touches including a sundeck, private sauna, steam bath and guided walking tours of the city, there is plenty to make guests feel special.

Meanwhile, selected VIP amenities are also available by arrangement, from massages, luxury picnics and limousines, to valet parking, babysitting and even hot air balloon rides.

When it comes to refreshment, on the other hand, it is no secret that Belgium is home to some of the most heavenly, fabulously ruinous food and drink on the planet, and Hotel Heritage does little to dispel this reputation. The in-house restaurant, Le Mystique, serves local Belgian and Flanders specialities including Duroc bacon, codfish, venison and, yes, a range of chocolate and patisserie items so delicious and guilt-inducing it could make grown men weep. And with a wine list featuring classic and contemporary labels from Continental Europe, it does not take long to warm to this place. Indeed, with its central location in the heart of this UNESCO World Heritage site, the so-called Venice of the North, Hotel Heritage serves as an authentic Flemish escape from the hectic streets and tourist hotspots of this famously reductive medieval city. And as with its Relais & Châteaux contemporaries around the world, every visitor is guaranteed exceptional service, lavishly appointed accommodation and ethereally fine cuisine. In fact, the one characteristic these 500-odd independent hotels have in common, somewhat paradoxically, is that they are all utterly unique. **BHS**

JOHAN AND ISABELLE CREYTENS

Meeting for the first time in 1991, project manager Johan and English teacher Isabelle Creytens shared a dream of running their own business. Spotting and later purchasing a desolate but utterly captivating property in the city centre, the newlyweds set about transforming it into a boutique hotel. Assisted by a committed tribe of craftsmen, plumbers, electricians and stone masons, they reopened the 19th-century mansion as a three-star Hansa Hotel in August 1993. With no previous experience in hospitality, both Johan and Isabelle proceeded to juggle a series of educational courses with the care of their three young children and the day-to-day running of their growing enterprise. Embracing modern technology and changing the name to Hotel Heritage along the way, they have over the last two decades succeeded in turning this historic building into an iconic urban retreat.

ARIA HOTEL
Prague, Czech Republic

Set in the heart of the city, just steps away from the Charles Bridge and St Nicholas Cathedral, Prague's best-kept secret is a revelation for explorers and food lovers alike.

Located within walking distance of the castle, Old Town Square and many more of this beloved city's most acclaimed landmarks, the Aria Hotel's musically themed suites are an irresistible attraction to both fans and philistines. Designed by Italian architects Rocco Magnoli and Lorenzo Carmellini, best known for their work with fashion legend Gianni Versace, this formerly modest, grey complex was transformed into a fascinating music-themed hotel in 2003.

Spread over four floors, the 51 guestrooms are each dedicated to four specific genres: Contemporary, Classical, Opera and Jazz. The musical legends receiving homage include Brahms, Bernstein, Elvis Presley, Ella Fitzgerald, Louis Armstrong, the Beatles, Maria Callas and Mozart. Billed as the presidential suite, the latter is dedicated to the eponymous

genius who first visited Prague as a child. With two bedrooms, adjacent bathrooms, a living area and exceptional views, a night here is reason alone to visit the city. Indeed, once ensconced, it will require a significant degree of willpower to extricate oneself from the suite's considerable comforts and charms.

Meanwhile, ranking highly among the city's finest dining destinations, Coda Restaurant represents a particular highlight for guests. With its art deco interior, imaginative menu and magnificent cityscape, this gourmet showcase – overseen by executive chef David Šašek – serves innovative dishes with a notable focus on employing the unusual *sous-vide* cooking method.

Of course, no tour of the Czech capital would be complete, or fulfilled, without a visit to the Vrtba, Prague's oldest and

best-known baroque gardens. This UNESCO World Heritage site is located directly next to the hotel and is accessible to guests via their own private entrance. This in itself demonstrates a level of exclusivity normally reserved for visitors with blue blood in their veins; at Aria Prague, everyone is treated like royalty.

A beautifully appointed, convenient and comfortable retreat from the tourist crowds, this delightful establishment has been the recipient of several international accolades in recent years, including TripAdvisor's 'Most Luxurious Hotel in the Czech Republic' in 2015; proof, if it were needed, that when true classical tradition meets exceptional contemporary style, both virtues may occasionally emerge triumphant. **BHS**

51 ROOMS GARDEN GYM MUSIC SALON ROOFTOP TERRACE SCREENING ROOM WINTER GARDEN

ARIA HOTEL PRAGUE, TRŽIŠTE 9, 118 00 PRAGUE, CZECH REPUBLIC
+420 225 334 111 | STAY@ARIA.CZ | WWW.ARIA.CZ

CHATEAU HERÁLEC
BOUTIQUE HOTEL AND SPA BY L'OCCITANE
Herálec, Czech Republic

Chateau Herálec's history is as much a part of its character and spirit as its sprawling grounds, boundless interior and iconic twin turrets.

This imposing, ludicrously pretty fairy-tale castle has been meticulously restored and transformed into a luxury boutique hotel, complete with the country's only L'Occitane spa.

19 ROOMS AND SUITES   BABYSITTING SERVICES   CINEMA   FINNISH SAUNA   GYM
HOT TUB   PLAYGROUND   POOL   RESTAURANT   SPA BY L'OCCITANE

CHATEAU HERÁLEC, HERÁLEC 1, 582 55 HERÁLEC, CZECH REPUBLIC
+420 569 669 111 | RECEPTION@CHATEAUHERALEC.COM | WWW.CHATEAUHERALEC.TRAVEL

BOUTIQUE
HOTEL    136   EUROPE
SELECTION

Recently lauded by TripAdvisor as one of the world's top-10 castle hotels, Chateau Herálec sits amid a striking landscape of forests and pastures in the verdant Vysočina area of the Czech Republic. Famous for its numerous UNESCO World Heritage historical monuments and resplendent with mountains, greenery and terracotta-coloured rooftops, the region is popular year-round with tourists and visitors seeking a peaceful escape in the Czech countryside.

Inside, there is a palpable sense of the detail and care employed by the craftsmen who carried out the restoration, from the original archways and the paintings of Czech artist Jan Honsa in the Standard Doubles, to Václava Kroupa's vast mural landscapes in a typical Luxury Double. With a total of 19 rooms and suites, the castle's interior is characterized by expansive, uncluttered, beautifully designed spaces, each unique and distinctive in its own way.

Move upwards in size, facilities and stature towards the Grande Suites, and the extravagance levels increase exponentially. From the medieval bath of the sizeable Presidential Suite of the Lords of Solms, to the noble flagship King's Suite of Lords Trčka from Lípa – every one of the rooms here has a story to tell.

Situated in the oldest part of the building, the castle's restaurant showcases the best of traditional regional cuisine and is a monument to the slow-food movement. Using fresh ingredients to produce modern takes on authentic recipes, the chef and his team hand-prepare dishes, including local specialities

such as Bohdaneč calvados, kulajda soup and roasted beef ribs with cabbage pies. Accompanied by one of the largest collections of branded Bordeaux wines in the country, the food here – in particular the tasting menus – brings a European flavour to a very Czech experience.

Meanwhile, as the first-ever licensee for a L'Occitane wellness spa in the Czech Republic, Chateau Herálec broke new boundaries in its quest to provide a five-star all-inclusive resort. Featuring Biosynchron technology – a pioneering treatment based on the principles of dry thermo and pulsating magnetic therapy – the facility is widely considered to be one of the best in the country. With a

swimming pool, Finnish sauna, Jacuzzi, massage room and fully equipped gym, a few days' immersion here will be as refreshing and invigorating as a few nights' dining in the hotel restaurant is entertaining and indulgent.

With its medieval underpinnings, vast grounds and abundant period detailing, Chateau Herálec's history is as much a part of its character and spirit as its sprawling grounds, boundless interior and iconic twin turrets. This utterly captivating castle may have been originally constructed in the 13th century, yet today it is there to be enjoyed in all its modern grandeur, complemented in large part by the charm of epochs past. BHS

THE CAPITAL HOTEL

London, England

Situated tantalizingly close to Harrods and enhanced by one of the city's finest fish restaurants, this family-run establishment is a paradigm of comfort for weary travellers.

For any potential visitor to the Big Smoke, the act of finding, appraising and selecting a hotel surely ranks among the most bemusing of challenges. Of the 120,000-plus rooms currently available, roughly two-thirds are located within 10 kilometres of Central London, leaving prospective guests with a significant and often daunting degree of choice. For those who select the Capital Hotel, however, a trip here is all but guaranteed to work out as planned. A restored Georgian townhouse in the heart of Knightsbridge, this five-star retreat's accommodation covers the entire spectrum. While the newly refurbished Classic Queen rooms are aimed at the solo traveller, the Classic King rooms – complete with large windows, twin beds and optional interconnectivity – cater for families and friends. Further up the scale, the Junior Suites offer spacious double or twin rooms, large windows and Nespresso coffee machines, and are perfect for long-stay guests or indeed those with overbearingly heavy shopping bags. Finally, the Studio and One-Bedroom Apartments represent the apogee of accommodation at The Capital. Benefitting from their own private entrance right next to the world's most famous department store, they occupy a uniquely privileged position; it doesn't get more exclusive than this.

Traditionally, any attempts to map out sightseeing itineraries often end in a kind of exhausted resignation, such is London's bewildering line-up of landmarks and visitor attractions. Fortunately, the Capital Hotel provides a welcoming retreat in which to camouflage oneself from the relentless buzz and frivolity of the streets outside. With its warm, familial atmosphere, beautifully appointed rooms and unspeakably delicious afternoon teas, the hotel presents a peerless blend of friendliness and professionalism, comfort and indulgence. As its social centre point, the Capital Bar offers a disarmingly impressive collection of cocktails, whiskies, champagne and cognacs, in addition to a well-stocked cellar of exceptional wines. Produced at the host's family winery in the Loire Valley, several labels play leading roles in the Michelin-Starred experience of chef Nathan Outlaw's eponymous eatery. As much a part of the hotel as it is a standalone miracle of contemporary cuisine, this astonishing seafood restaurant sources the freshest fish direct from boats off the Cornish coast. With set lunches, tasting menus, whisky dinners, masterclasses and private dining, there is plenty here to keep gastronomes, bon vivants and food buffs busy for the duration of their stay. BHS

49 ROOMS AND EIGHT SUITES | BAR | RESTAURANT

THE CAPITAL HOTEL, 22–24 BASIL STREET, KNIGHTSBRIDGE, LONDON SW3 1AT, UNITED KINGDOM
+ 44 207 589 5171 | RESERVATIONS@CAPITALHOTEL.CO.UK | WWW.CAPITALHOTEL.CO.UK

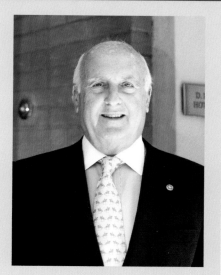

DAVID LEVIN

Fired by an enthusiasm for hotels and leisure from an early age, David is an illustrious pioneer of many modern initiatives, innovations and standards within British hospitality. Revolutionizing the sector in the mid-1960s with the creation of the UK's first gastro-pub, the Royal Oak, in Yattendon, Berkshire, in 1971 he went on to launch the Capital, in Knightsbridge. A 'grand hotel in miniature', this iconic establishment quickly became the blueprint for the future of boutique properties in the UK and beyond. Running the business to this day alongside daughter Kate, David was honoured in 2016 with an MBE for youth training and services to hospitality.

Full of intricate, traditional detailing and complemented by one of the highest-rated restaurants in Estonia, Villa Ammende manages to vividly re-create the atmosphere of a wealthy merchant's home at the turn of the 20th century.

Originally built as a Baltic Coast summer holiday home and wedding venue for a wealthy German inheritor, Villa Ammende occupies a special place in Estonia's history. Completed in 1905 and sold by the family a quarter of a century later, the house enjoyed a variety of uses in the intervening decades. Since undergoing a meticulous two-year restoration and reopening as a hotel and restaurant in 1999, it is now recognized as the area's most luxurious establishment and one of only three genuine Art Nouveau hotels in the world.

With space for up to 35 people spread throughout two buildings, the accommodation comprises 18 ultra-luxurious suites and rooms, all of which showcase unique interior design, original-style furniture and quite spectacular attention to detail. Welcomed into the high-ceilinged grand entrance hall by staff in formal dress and accompanied on a guided tour of the accommodation,

visitors take a step back in time to a bygone era. Varying in size rather than quality and facilities, the suites and rooms all follow a familiar line. From the sauna and balcony of the flagship Ammende Suite, to the Mahogany Suite's bathroom-Jacuzzi and balcony overlooking the landscaped gardens, it is all reminiscent of how things used to be for the affluent classes.

Similarly, the Filoori beauty salon provides a range of traditional and contemporary therapies, including massages, facials and laser-guided skin treatments, some of which are also available in the suites and bedrooms themselves.

Equipped with no fewer than three dining areas, a spacious terrace and exquisitely maintained landscaped gardens, the feel throughout of old-fashioned art nouveau – updated with modern amenities for the 21st century – is bewitchingly nostalgic.

Outside, the white sands of Pärnu Beach are only a short walk away, and not much farther down the road lies the

town centre, with its high-end shopping precinct and famous concert hall.

Full of intricate, traditional detailing and complemented by one of the highest-rated restaurants in Estonia, Villa Ammende manages to vividly re-create the atmosphere of a wealthy merchant's home at the turn of the 20th century.

With its authentic art nouveau paintings, wood carvings, candelabra, antiques and hunting trophies, the property deftly combines the feel of a luxurious modern guesthouse with traditional old-fashioned elegance. Ideal for romantic weekends, gourmet vacations and relaxing holidays, it is a step back in time to a bourgeois era when material wealth matched manners, quality and refinement; it is also why, in addition to reflecting Estonia's colourful past, the historic hotel occupies a distinctive place in this remarkable country's present. BHS

CHÂTEAU DE LA RESLE

Burgundy, France

A fresh, immaculate, über-cool countryside retreat that teems with art and homely charm in one of the most famous wine regions in the world.

Think of a French rural château, and the chances are it resembles one you've seen before on a hot day in the lush, sweet-smelling French countryside: wrought-iron gates; a grand driveway; manicured grounds; a long white or grey or sandstone-coloured building with perhaps a couple of ancient barns alongside; above all, an unmistakable air of unadulterated, extraordinary elegance. We've all seen them, and we know what they look like, sure as the first British-style house we all drew as kids had four windows and a front door.

Whatever the size, whatever the location, there is something about these domestic castles that begs to be discovered: an alluring, often paradoxical historical blend of romance and conflict; of amusement and sadness; of battles and innocence; of history and contemporary beauty. Impressive in stature and footprint, but often sufficiently compact to play host to a modern home, they hold about them a level of intrigue that most domestic dwellings couldn't begin to emulate. This is exactly what springs to mind when Château de la Resle is discovered for the first time. A beautifully restored manor house with grounds containing exquisite art pieces from the owners' private collection, this 18th-century marvel contains two guest rooms and four individually designed suites. Proprietors Johan and Pieter, two gentlemen with a sharp eye for design and detail, have clearly spent considerable time and resources restoring the château and its attendant buildings. From the intimacy and warmth of the bedrooms to the precise care of the minutiae in the open spaces, living areas and grounds, Château de la Resle is considerably more than the sum of its many beautiful parts.

Perhaps inevitably, food and drink take centre stage, and dining here is always something of a surprise; with no fixed menu, the dishes vary depending on the availability of fresh ingredients on any given day. Johan's role as head chef ensures a resolute commitment, where possible, to the use of fresh, organic, locally grown produce to prepare a range of classic and contemporary French-style

4 SUITES AND 2 ROOMS   GYM   HEATED OUTDOOR POOL   RESTAURANT   SAUNA   SPA   STEAM BATH

CHÂTEAU DE LA RESLE, LIEU-DIT LA RESLE, RUE DES BUTTES, 89230 MONTIGNY-LA-RESLE, FRANCE
+33 6 86 11 29 22 | INFO@CHATEAUDELARESLE.COM | WWW.CHATEAUDELARESLE.COM

dishes. Studiously avoiding the tired clichés of giblets and frog legs, he instead favours more traditional creations such as free-range chicken, a leg of slow-cooked lamb with fresh vegetables or sustainably caught sea bass on a bed of oven-baked potatoes.

For dessert, diners are presented with a diverse choice including fruit crumble, panna cotta or a chocolate tart with homemade ice-cream and followed, on occasion, by the requisite selection of authentic French cheeses. There is no chance of ever leaving here hungry.

So, yes, while many rural châteaux may look similar from the outside, a great many more stand out. Of these, a few may have long-since been deserted, some are still in the hands of illustrious families with colourful histories and a good many others are available for hire or holiday rent. The notable difference between all of them and Château de la Resle, however, is that the latter is perfect in every possible way. **BHS**

MÈZE MAISON

Languedoc, France

A painstakingly renovated 19th-century former wine merchant's home, Mèze Maison lies at the heart of a vibrant seaside port in the Languedoc wine region of the south of France. Throw open the hefty doors and it quickly becomes clear how much effort went into the restoration; high ceilings and exposed wooden beams are complemented by antique mirrors and intricate chandeliers, while the individually designed rooms are notably bespoke. Intended as a home-from-home experience and equipped with huge beds, Egyptian cotton sheets, exposed beams and traditional wood panelling, it is strikingly unique.

High in the attic and with space for three guests, the spacious, characterful Clara suite showcases original oak beams, ensuite shower and stunning views of the town's château and gardens. On the

This harbourside guest house provides comforting luxury and a home-like charm in the ancient southern village of Mèze.

4 ROOMS BAR BEACH CHÂTEAU VIEWS COMPLIMENTARY BICYCLES AND HELMETS WEDDINGS

MÈZE MAISON, 2 RUE FRANÇOIS BESSE, 34140 MÈZE, FRANCE
+33 0621 16 43 42 | ROB@MEZEMAISON.COM | WWW.MEZEMAISON.COM

same floor, Mimi's twin beds may either be kept separate or joined together to form a Superking-size double. With high-beamed ceilings, freestanding bath and separate ensuite shower, this is the perfect accommodation for friends or couples.

Meanwhile, one level down, Jo-Jo also includes views of the château and gardens, in addition to a private balcony and ensuite dressing-room with shower. And for the most spacious, luxurious room of all, Louis's floor-to-ceiling French windows, private balconies, Superking-size double bed and freestanding bathtub place it resolutely in a class of its own.

Following a complimentary evening aperitif in the airy salon, a wander along the harbour is recommended. With a variety of cafés and restaurants nearby, many specializing in fresh fish, oysters and

mussels, the town's layout renders private transport largely redundant. Consequently, Picpoul de Pinet – the local dry white wine – may be enjoyed in whichever quantity suits the prevailing mood.

As it happens, Mèze's proximity to tourist attractions, cultural diversions and sporting facilities is arguably one of its greatest assets. In addition to private catamaran tours of the oyster beds and sailing and kite-surfing lessons in the nearby lagoon, there are a host of other interests within an hour's drive of the guesthouse. Of these, the natural thermal baths in Balaruc are especially popular. Likewise, the hilltop town of Roquebrun is a must-visit for both swimming and kayaking, while Bouzigues' reputation as the home of the French oyster means the 20-minute bike ride is effectively compulsory for every foodie.

A little further on, the Abbaye de Valmagne attracts a large number of history lovers, many of whom no doubt come in search of the 13th-century abbey's home-produced beer and wine. Fans of art and drama, on the other hand, flock to van Gogh's former home in Arles, while Molière devotees tend to descend on Pézenas, where the playwright once stayed with his theatre group, l'Illustre Théâtre.

Together with Sète's summer jazz festival, the leafy squares and outdoor cafés of Montpellier, and Nîmes' Roman amphitheatre, the biggest challenge for visitors to this area will be to determine their own itinerary. The one certainty, however, will be a warm welcome and outstanding hospitality at Mèze Maison. **BHS**

BIG BLUE BEACH VILLA

Mykonos, Greece

Live like a billionaire in this sprawling luxury villa with private beach on the mesmerizing island of Mykonos.

Developer/contractor: Andreas Metaxa
Architects: www.kokkinoukourkoulas.com/en
Interior Designer: Anna-Maria Coscoros
www.amcoscoros.com
Engineer: Gerasimos Vasilatos

From its intensely restful spot overlooking the Aegean Sea and neighbouring archipelago, this outstanding villa inspires guests to exploit its facilities. With 5,000 square metres of landscaped grounds and private access to a sandy beach down below, there is more than sufficient space to spread out and feel free.

The four ensuite bedrooms in the main house are all blessed with incredible views, and the master suite is equipped with an atrium, walk-in closet, bathroom, whirlpool and private garden with seating area. Unusually for a holiday home there is a further bedroom for a maid or nanny that comes in handy for those hoping to renounce ownership of offspring for the duration of the holiday.

With plenty of facilities and activities including a gymnasium, indoor and outdoor cinemas and swimming pool, the villa has abundant distractions to keep guests busy. While water sports and boat tours will attract the more adventurous types, the villa and its grounds are so spacious and appealing that engagement and entertainment of some sort is always on offer.

Full of olive trees, flowers and aromatic herbs, the grounds provide fairytale-style adventure for children,

SLEEPS 14   BUTLER SERVICE   CHILD-FRIENDLY   GARDEN PAVILION   GYMNASIUM
INFINITY POOL WITH SEA VIEWS   POOL BAR AND TERRACE   PRIVATE BEACH

BIG BLUE BEACH VILLA, DIAKOFTIS, AGHIOS GIANNIS, MYKONOS, CYCLADES, GREECE
+44 208 672 7040 | INFO@MYPRIVATEVILLAS.COM

while the extensive terraces, infinity pool and pergola-covered seating areas will satisfy sociable adults. And for those keen to expend minimal effort devising and serving drinks and meals, the optional butler service is the ideal accompaniment to the large dining-room and outdoor seating areas.

A magnet both for bacchanalian party types and those seeking shelter from the wilder side of this famously upbeat holiday island, Mykonos is well-known for its contrasting lifestyles. Striking a masterly balance between beauty and hedonism, tranquillity and entertainment, this peaceful, beguiling, ultimately irresistible destination always has something to say for itself.

And in the middle of it all, the Big Blue Beach Villa provides a sublime environment in which to take advantage of this beautiful island's light-hearted and liberated way of life. BHS

AENAON VILLAS

Santorini, Greece

*Traditional Greek hospitality meets clifftop views, luxurious accommodation
and achingly beautiful sunsets in this romantic hillside retreat.*

6 VILLAS   BAR   BUTLER SERVICE   CALDERA VIEWS   INFINITY POOL   WEDDINGS

AENAON VILLAS, IMEROVIGLI, SANTORINI 84700, CYCLADES, GREECE
+30 22860 27014 | INFO@AENAONVILLAS.GR | WWW.AENAONVILLAS.GR

BOUTIQUE
HOTEL   149   EUROPE
SELECTION

Located at the highest, narrowest point of Santorini, these glorious private villas sit on separate levels overlooking both the East and West side of the Aegean Sea. Constructed from whitewashed indigenous volcanic stone near an ancient path that connects the nearby towns and villages, Aenaon has literally been carved out of the side of the mountain. By way of illustration, a click on the hotel's website confirms that this place presents arguably the most arresting sea-view setting in the Northern Hemisphere. An aerial shot of the loftiest villa and its attendant panoramas, the single photograph captures just how spectacular Aenaon's location really is.

Beautifully appointed, the majority of its six villas are equipped with Queen-size bed, generous living space with private veranda and the requisite views of either the Aegean Sea or the caldera. If a larger living area is a consideration, both Feggeri and Elidami benefit from additional space, with the latter also enjoying its own private plunge pool. However, at more than twice the size of its siblings, Villa Marily provides a master bed and two smaller rooms, in addition to a living-dining area and large veranda. Pure white surfaces and furnishings abound, contrasted in the bathrooms with black volcanic shower tiles; the overarching effect is one of immaculate minimalism and effortless style, and it all adds up to a profoundly luxurious experience.

Outside, the hotel's infinity pool is recessed deep into expansive terraces looking out over the caldera and the surrounding mountains. If local sightseeing is a priority, a wander along the ancient path to nearby Oia is well worth the effort. With its cobbled side streets, seafood restaurants and numerous trinket shops, this pretty little town quickly endears itself to visitors. And if a change of clothes is available, a skip down the steps for a dip in Ammoudi Bay also comes highly recommended.

Family-run, the hotel is undoubtedly the island's finest boutique retreat and in common with the Greek holiday experience in general, the welcome and service are as warm as the Santorini sunshine. By all means visit at the earliest opportunity but be prepared to abandon any plans for exploration further afield; once encountered, Aenaon is nigh impossible to forget. **BHS**

GIORGOS AND ALEXANDRA ALEXIOU

Having yearned for years to open their own boutique hotel, Giorgos and Alexandra eventually made their dream a reality. Using his expertise in engineering, architecture and environmental studies to design the entire space themselves, in 2009 they began the project that would eventually become Aenaon Villas. Utilizing the island's ancient volcanic stone, the construction team created the instantly recognisable complex of luxurious whitewashed hillside villas, and in doing so proved that heritage and tradition may coexist in harmony with luxury and modernity. Heading up the family business – their daughters Maria Christina and Elly Lydia often join them during the holidays – the couple command a small team of friendly but professional staff who are adept at being discreetly present when required and all but invisible when not. After all, in this particular establishment, peace and absolute privacy are key.

ARIA HOTEL

Budapest, Hungary

This bright, warm, well-positioned property is just a couple of minutes' walk from St Stephen's Basilica and affords spectacular nightscapes of Hungary's largest city.

44 ROOMS AND 5 SUITES POOL ROOF GARDEN SKY-BAR SPA WINE-AND-CHEESE RECEPTION

ARIA HOTEL BUDAPEST, HERCEGPRÍMÁS UTCA 5, BUDAPEST H-1051, HUNGARY
+36 144 54 055 | STAY@ARIAHOTELBUDAPEST.COM | WWW.ARIAHOTELBUDAPEST.COM

BOUTIQUE HOTEL SELECTION 152 EUROPE

situated near the world-famous Chain Bridge, the Aria Hotel is complemented by its association with this iconic landmark, the first permanent platform connecting Buda and Pest. Suspended across the River Danube, the structure looks as timeless and beguiling today as it did when it was built in the late 1800s. Fortunately, the hotel's exterior is sufficiently decorous and refined to be enhanced, rather than overshadowed, by the bridge's presence.

Continuing the musical theme of other properties in the Aria family, the 49 bedrooms are supplemented by deliciously quirky design details: violins hang from the hotel's Stradivari Restaurant; harps stand in as lighting fixtures; and a piano-key marble pathway leads to the Music Garden courtyard, like a tuneful Yellow Brick Road. The hotel's famous centrepiece, this stunning rooftop enclosure is the first of its kind in Europe and the ideal venue in which to socialize, dine and admire the cityscapes. Affording guests a clear, comfortable, climate-controlled view of the sky, whatever the season, the Music Garden represents the only feasible scenario where a glass ceiling will fail to prevent anyone moving up in the world . . .

In common with Aria sister establishments, each of the Budapest hotel's four wings is dedicated to a specific music genre: Classical, Opera, Contemporary and Jazz. Adorned with caricatures created by internationally acclaimed artist Joseph Blecha, the rooms and suites aim to celebrate the world's greatest musical legends, including Maria Callas, Count Basie, Bob Dylan, James Brown and Hungary's own Franz Liszt.

Nearby, the four Opera parlours – Romeo & Juliet, Carmen, Madama Butterfly and the La Traviata Terrace – are ideal for use as meeting rooms or hospitality suites. Furnished with sofa-bed, dining table and kitchenette, these smaller spaces may be combined with a bedroom to form a Duet Suite, or with two bedrooms to create the perfect solution for families.

Meanwhile, Harmony Spa's swimming pool, hot tub, Jacuzzi and sauna add to a long list of rather fabulous treatments, including massages, facials, detoxes, body wraps and rooftop yoga. As previous European winners at the World Boutique Hotel Awards for its spa facility, the team at Aria Budapest provide unique, musically inspired rituals to help guests relax and de-stress after a restless day's sightseeing and touring. And with the landscaped rooftop High Note SkyBar available for sunbathing, pre-dinner cocktails and dining, guests may sit back and drink in the city's unmistakable sights, sounds and aromas.

Showcasing the underlying musical theme of this diverse, historic, engrossing short-break destination, Aria Budapest embraces visitors with its engaging combination of warm welcome, exceptional facilities and personalized service. BHS

ION LUXURY ADVENTURE HOTEL

Nesjavellir, Iceland

Relax in a geothermal pool and drink in the magic of the Northern Lights from this remote rural escape just an hour outside Reykjavík.

45 ROOMS   ECO SUPER-JEEP TOURS   GLACIER HIKE   GYM   HELICOPTER TOURS
NATURAL SPA   OUTDOOR GEOTHERMAL POOL   RIDING   SAUNA

ION LUXURY ADVENTURE HOTEL, NESJAVELLIR, 801 SELFOSS, ICELAND
+354 482 3415 | RESERVATIONS@IONICELAND.IS | WWW.IONICELAND.IS

BOUTIQUE HOTEL SELECTION   155   EUROPE

The 45 rooms, each with dramatic views of either the Nesjavellir Geothermal Power Plant or the desolate lava fields of the UNESCO-listed Thingvellir National Park, are plush with modern refinements and amenities.

A chic minimalist establishment set against a striking backdrop of mountains, geysers and waterfalls, ION Luxury Adventure Hotel is, quite literally, in a world of its own. Situated close to the Golden Circle – the popular travel route in the south of the island – it is the perfect base from which to explore Iceland's rich heritage and extreme-adventure opportunities. The 45 rooms, each with dramatic views of either the Nesjavellir Geothermal Power Plant or the desolate lava fields of the UNESCO-listed Thingvellir National Park, are plush with modern refinements and amenities. Featuring hypoallergenic beds, environmentally friendly showers and, in Deluxe variants, floor-to-ceiling windows, the accommodation provides a cushion of comfort after a day's exploration in one of the most arresting, fascinating habitats on Earth.

Meanwhile, the spa's, extensive treatment menu and outdoor pool all help to rejuvenate guests after a challenging glacier trek or an icy afternoon's fly-fishing. With body scrubs, massages, facials and multiple therapies for hands and feet, there is every chance to rest and recuperate.

Thankfully, the hotel's restaurant continues the theme of sympathetic buffer to the wilderness outside. With several varieties of ultra-fresh Arctic char, salmon and cod on the menu, Silfra serves up seasonal, contemporary dishes with a noticeable emphasis on sustainable, farm-fresh ingredients. Adopting modern Nordic styles of cuisine, lead chefs Hrafnkell Sigríðarson and Hafsteinn Ólafsson subscribe to the slow-food style of cooking and the results, particularly in this setting, are spectacular. It is not mere hyperbole to claim that this exceptional restaurant is a culinary oasis in a dystopian desert.

Even still, it is the jaw-dropping, award-winning Northern Lights bar that really grabs guests by the lapels. Featuring a seemingly infinite range of craft beers, liqueurs and spirits from Iceland's multiple, celebrated microbreweries, this is a beacon of light in a dark, foreboding, thoroughly captivating landscape. Quite simply, when the swirling green solar winds of the Aurora Borealis are in full flicker, there is no better place from which to witness this world-famous phenomenon. ION Luxury Adventure Hotel is, effectively, the IMAX® of Iceland. BHS

SIGURLAUG SVERRISDÓTTIR

Having explored much of the world in her former career with a charter airline, in 2010 Sigurlaug drew on her extensive travel experience to expand her burgeoning training company into adventure tours. Establishing ION three years later, she sought to create a luxury destination that offered a taste of true Icelandic culture through a combination of nature, fashion, music, food and wine. From the volcanic marvels of Mount Hengill to the urban sophistication of Reykjavik, the country's unique landscape played a pivotal role in the design of the 45-room hotel. Built primarily on the principles of sustainable business, eco-tourism and the natural features of the island, this warm, luxurious, unmistakable establishment encourages guests to discover and celebrate the wilderness around them. Indeed, it is this underlying philosophy that inspired ION's very motto: 'Where everything meets nothing'.

COOLMORE MANOR HOUSE

County Donegal, Ireland

This 19th-century Georgian country house in Ireland's rugged, untamed north-west has been meticulously restored and transformed into a homely exclusive-use retreat.

3 ROOMS AND 1 APARTMENT   BAR   BEACH   COOKING SERVICES*   HELIPAD   MASSAGES

OPTIONAL BED AND BREAKFAST*   SAUNA AND HOT TUB   SELF-CATERING   SPA   SHOW-JUMPING HORSE STUD

* BY SEPARATE ARRANGEMENT.

COOLMORE MANOR HOUSE, ROSSNOWLAGH, CO. DONEGAL, F94 K7W7, IRELAND
+353 71 985 9997 | INFO@COOLMOREMANORHOUSE.COM | WWW.COOLMOREMANORHOUSE.COM

BOUTIQUE HOTEL SELECTION   158   EUROPE

Set in five hectares of pastureland on the Wild Atlantic Way, Coolmore Manor was originally constructed as a house for the local laird and later converted into an eight-bedroom hotel. After falling into disrepair, this imposing structure was acquired by its current owners in 2011 following a partial restoration, and in the intervening years it has been fully renovated and refurbished. Now rated a five-star luxury retreat and blessed with a tasteful blend of period furnishings and contemporary art, it is as homely as a country cottage and the warm, comfortable interior belies its rugged surroundings. All three ensuite double bedrooms enjoy ocean views of Donegal Bay, taking in both the long sandy stretch of Rossnowlagh Beach and Slieve League in the foreground, and the Blue Stack Mountains behind. A living-room, study, kitchen, dining-room and conservatory complete the public areas, and there is generous space to accommodate six people in comfort.

Showcasing several period features including high stucco ceilings, flagstone floors, marble sills and sash windows with original wooden shutters, the rooms benefit from all modern amenities while retaining their notable original features and character. Should the need arise, the property's former coach house may be hired as an additional two-person apartment, while if relaxation is a key consideration, Coolmore Manor's state-of-the-art treatment room and accompanying therapies will reset the mind and purge stress from the soul. With a full and varied programme of remedies including physiotherapy, hot stones, massages, seaweed baths and pain therapies, there is a treatment to suit most common aches, pains and ailments. Likewise, the natural heat and ocean views from newly added sauna and hot tub are sufficiently stimulating to soothe stiff muscles and cramping calves.

Outside, the striking Georgian architecture is set against a stark backdrop of untamed moors, roiling seascapes and windswept cliffs. A short jaunt around the back of the property reveals the iconic Bellavista's near 360-degree views over Donegal Bay, while further around the coast, Slieve League in Donegal shows off the highest sea cliffs in Europe.

With several of Ireland's best-known golf courses located nearby, the outdoors life at Coolmore is as exciting as the inside is comforting. And the quiet, intensely pretty scenery also makes this an excellent starting point for hikes and outdoor excursions, although beware the risk of misinterpreting the forecast and failing to dress for the occasion; the countryside out here may be beautiful to behold but it takes no prisoners when the weather turns. While such warnings may sound like scaremongering, the potential for foreboding actually makes Coolmore Manor House even more alluring. For, at the end of a long day exploring the local hills and ancient villages, there is nothing more satisfying than congregating around the fireplace or in the warmth of the farmhouse-style kitchen, whisky in hand, while the Wild Atlantic Way lives up to its name outside. **BHS**

CLARE ISLAND LIGHTHOUSE

County Mayo, Ireland

Perched on the edge of an island off the coast of County Mayo, this converted former lighthouse encourages guests to reconnect with nature.

6 ROOMS   SMALL WEDDINGS   CLIFFTOP VIEWS

CLARE ISLAND LIGHTHOUSE, BALLYTOUGHEY, CLARE ISLAND, CLEW BAY, CO. MAYO, IRELAND
+353 87 668 9758 | INFO@CLAREISLANDLIGHTHOUSE.COM | WWW.CLAREISLANDLIGHTHOUSE.COM

A customary highlight for guests is a six-course dinner served on a mahogany dining table around which everyone gathers, a quirk which adds to the convivial atmosphere.

Accessed by a 20-minute ferry ride across the Wild Atlantic Way, Clare Island is as unspoiled now as it was when medieval monks constructed its abbey in the 13th century. Comprehensively and sympathetically restored, the 200-year-old renovated clifftop retreat now boasts six bedrooms, each of which combines modern amenities with original period features. From open fires and flagstone floors to double-glazed windows and jet-black painted balustrades, the mix of old and new is as seamless as the weather outside is wild.

A pre-dinner stroll or cycle is (usually) recommended, and the 120-metre cliffs nearby provide the perfect platform from which to breathe in the brackish sea air. It is a formidable view whatever the conditions, with snow-covered mountains, wild vegetation and panoramic seascapes all jostling for supremacy on the horizon.

Back at base guests are invited to share an aperitif in the drawing-room before heading through for dinner. A customary highlight for guests is the six-course dinner served on the mahogany dining table around which everyone gathers, a quirk which adds to the convivial atmosphere. Indeed, with a piano, well-stocked library and a notable absence of television, the door at Clare Island Lighthouse is forever open for good old-fashioned conversation between guests.

Of course, if solitude is key, there is always the outdoors, where the climate determines the itinerary and the landscape does most of the talking. And that encapsulates the soul of this particular destination: with a unique combination of exceptional food, the warmest hospitality and a range of arresting outdoor pursuits, it is a far cry from traditional island retreats. Our advice would be to discover it now, before everyone else does. BHS

RELAIS DI TENUTA SANTA CATERINA

Asti, Italy

This refined countryside retreat in Northern Italy's Piedmont hills prioritizes luxury and quietude, with a reassuring emphasis on fine wines from the surrounding region.

6 SUITES · BUTLER SERVICE · COOKING COURSES · GOLF · MASSAGE · SPA · SWIMMING POOL · WINE-TASTING · YOGA

RELAIS DI TENUTA SANTA CATERINA, VIA GUGLIELMO MARCONI 17, 14035 GRAZZANO BADOGLIO AT, ITALY
+39 0141 925472 | RELAIS@TENUTA-SANTA-CATERINA.IT | WWW.TENUTA-SANTA-CATERINA.IT

BOUTIQUE HOTEL SELECTION · 162 · EUROPE

It requires a certain kind of discerning, committed individual or group to seek out a holiday destination based on a single specific activity, discipline or interest. For adventurers and adrenalin junkies, pretty much every country and continent has something to offer; for sports fans, the same applies. Artists, archaeologists and music lovers, on the other hand, have a smaller but equally compelling pool from which to map out trips, itineraries and expeditions. And if food is the principal focus, most major cities are blessed with at least one standout establishment; indeed, entire nations have forged convincing reputations for their indigenous cuisine.

In contrast, only a handful of tourists are ever sufficiently fortunate to find themselves touring the wine region of their dreams, such is the exclusive nature of these destinations. This relative lack of universal popularity may be attributable to a variety of reasons, including cost,

accessibility and a perceived emphasis on the raw product rather than home comforts and amenities. Likewise, the local accommodation may fall short of emulating the quality of the wines on offer. Happily, however, there is one notable exception.

Hidden away in the rolling valleys of the UNESCO-listed Monferrato region of Northern Italy, Relais di Tenuta Santa Caterina is a boutique hotel with not one but several exceptional differences. Named after the winery's own labels, the six individually styled suites feature exclusive design details including Turkish baths and chromotherapy tubs, mini-pools, balconies and outstanding views. Among them, Setecàpita's private spa and Salidoro's leaf-shaped bathtub invite occupants to hide away from the world, while Silente's private balcony beseeches guests to savour the views of Jardin Clos. Meanwhile, Arlandino may be twinned with nearby Vignalina to make

a single, spacious apartment, and Navlè's 'mysterious, nocturnal' atmosphere completes the accommodation.

Acquired in 2003 by Milan lawyer Guido Carlo Alleva, the Santa Caterina estate subsequently underwent a decade-long, ground-up overhaul and refurbishment. Both the vineyard and its buildings were sympathetically restored, with Guido's daughter Giulia successfully blending tradition and modernity without compromising heritage and character. The result is a masterpiece, albeit one that represents only half the story. Almost 20 metres beneath the entrance hall lies the Infernotto, an underground vault containing Guido's own private wine collection of more than 5,000 bottles. And with swimming, riding, quad-biking and golfing all available nearby, this elegant country house presents a unique, deliciously inviting prospect for anyone seeking luxury and vinous Heaven. BHS

PUNTA TRAGARA

Capri, Italy

*Designed by Le Corbusier in the 1920s and overlooking the famous Faraglioni rocks,
this seminal five-star hotel occupies the most sought-after position on the island.*

38 ROOMS AND 6 SUITES   BAR   CLIFFTOP LOCATION   PANORAMIC SEA VIEWS   RESTAURANT   TWIN OUTDOOR POOLS

PUNTA TRAGARA, VIA TRAGARA 57, 80073 CAPRI, ITALY
+39 081 837 0844 | INFO@HOTELTRAGARA.IT | WWW.HOTELTRAGARA.COM

BOUTIQUE
HOTEL   164   EUROPE
SELECTION

A former holiday home that was transformed into a hotel in 1973, Punta Tragara has enjoyed extraordinary success in the intervening years. Located on the west-facing side of this magical isle, opposite the Gulf of Naples, this unbelievably pretty structure has seemingly been sculpted out of the cliff face, and its terracotta façade is arguably as distinctive as the views from its multiple terraces.

Contemporary, spacious and filled with light, the 44 recently redesigned guestrooms vary in design, décor and size but match each other for quality and home comforts. Each Double Prestige Garden View room features either a balcony or small private terrace overlooking the gardens and swimming pool, while the Double Superior Sea View room is equally blessed, in this case with views of Marina Piccola Bay. The six suites, on the other hand, include the spacious Tragara, the 65-square-metre Certosa, and the self-explanatory but no less spectacular Penthouse. All boast marble bathrooms, balconies or terraces and sea views over the Gulf of Naples and all, as expected, are sublime.

Meanwhile, the Unica Spa offers intense, high-performance treatments including the signature hydradermie face treatments, thalassotherapy and the Physio Lab. The two outdoor swimming pools – one naturally heated, the other via whirlpool jets – are genuinely beautiful to behold and of course play essential roles during the searing summer months.

Nearby, the 70-seat Monzù Restaurant's panoramic veranda seduces guests with views so distracting they carry serious potential for disrupting the flow of conversation during dinner. Fortunately, executive chef Luigi Lionetti is well aware of the competing forces vying for the attention of his diners, and uses his imaginative dishes to counter any such threat. Employing the freshest produce to prepare local and national specialities and favourites, he and his team effortlessly capture the essence of Capri life. Furthermore, the menu itself is accompanied by an extensive world-wide wine list of more than 200 labels. Happy to provide informal, knowledgeable commentary to assist with matching and pairing, staff may also discuss more esoteric suggestions with connoisseurs and committed wine buffs.

All this effort and meticulous planning is typical of the Punta Tragara way of life; the easy-going appearance belies the Herculean efforts and relentless attention to detail behind the scenes. For while this is, for many people, the most relaxed, luxurious and appealing establishment in southern Italy, the work that goes on in the background to maintain that position is nothing short of heroic. That, together with the warmest welcome and tortuously beautiful seascapes, is why the hotel continues to occupy a special place in the hearts of hundreds of privileged visitors from around the world. BHS

PALAZZO DEL VICE RE

Lake Como, Italy

*In the town of Lezzeno, just minutes from beautiful Bellagio and
far away from the madness of Milan, Palazzo del Vice Re sits
peacefully with fine cuisine, character and Lake Como at its heart.*

3 APARTMENTS, 1 SUITE AND 1 ROOM   BAR   BREAKFAST BUFFET   BUTLER SERVICE   PET-FRIENDLY   WEDDINGS

PALAZZO DEL VICE RE, LOCALITÀ PESCAÙ 51, LEZZENO 22025, ITALY
+39 031 914 628 | INFO@PALAZZODELVICERE.COM | WWW.PALAZZODELVICERE.COM

BOUTIQUE
HOTEL   166   EUROPE
SELECTION

A former aristocratic palace, this painstakingly restored property reopened in 2014 after being transformed into luxurious self-catering accommodation. Lead by staff down cobbled streets into the original 17th-century courtyard, complete with Doric columns and ancient well, it is easy to be confounded with the somewhat paradoxical appearance of the Palazzo; tall, handsome and distinctive, its dusty-orange façade is curiously as subtle as it is imposing – but it is nonetheless all the better for it. Comprising one-, two- and three-bedroom apartments, a junior suite and a luxury double room, the fastidiously detailed accommodation provides the highlight of this glorious lakeside destination, where old-world charm meets modern creature comforts.

Taking its name from the darker burnt-orange walls leading up to the timber ceiling, Il Fuoco is the first-floor luxury double room with Jacuzzi shower and large window offering plentiful natural light. And as the Palazzo's junior suite, La Vista, offers more than 61 square metres of antique furnishings, original frescoes, high ceilings and fine oriental rugs. With a marble bathroom and enchanting views of the lake and the snow-capped mountains beyond, it's like a window onto a different world. La Torre, on the other hand, is the spacious one-bedroom apartment featuring an open-plan living, dining and kitchen area. Looking out over a tree-filled park to the harbour and lake, the view is shared with the snow-capped mountains in the far distance.

Meanwhile, L'Isola Comacina is the Palazzo's vast two-bedroom apartment. Located on the first floor it overlooks the eponymous island on the far side of Lake Como and features original cotto floors, antique fireplace, timber beam ceilings, a pianoforte and a step-out balcony above the courtyard.

Finally, L'Onda is the flagship 158-square-metre three-bedroom loft apartment that takes its name from the little waves lapping at the shores below. Found at the top of the Palazzo's sweeping staircase, this room also benefits from an open-plan kitchen and living area and is large enough to accommodate five adults in comfort. However, it is the low-set windows that place this particular accommodation in a separate class of its own; from the comfort of the Jacuzzi, it is the perfect spot to watch the last vestiges of daylight disappear over the mountains. And if there's one sight worth seeing in Italy, it is sunset over Lake Como. BHS

HOTEL SPLENDIDE ROYAL

Rome, Italy

Based purely on the view from its elevated position overlooking St Peter's Basilica, Splendide Royal's Mirabelle Restaurant automatically qualifies as a contender for Best Restaurant in Rome. With vast glass terrace doors opening out onto a panoramic cityscape of unspeakable beauty, the seventh-floor establishment acts as a magnet for sophisticated Romans and discerning visitors. From the 19th-century palaces of Pinciano, Villa Medici and Trinità dei Monti, all the way to the Vatican and the Janiculum, there is a distinctly cinematic beauty to this sweeping urban vista, particularly at night. Boasting arguably the most elegant gourmet terrace in Rome, Mirabelle has long been an exclusive meeting point for the cognoscenti and

is considered by many to be among the finest such establishments in the world; moreover, the Mediterranean dishes of Executive Chef maestro Stefano Marzetti are widely acknowledged as being just as extraordinary as the setting in which they are served. Add to this the charming effect of the soft lighting and antique tableware – all augmented by the meticulous attention to detail that reflects the efforts of the kitchen team – and you have a recipe for a truly memorable evening.

However, while it doubtless provides a seductive attraction and is capable of luring the pleasure-seeker on the strength of its own merits, the restaurant tells only half the story. With its own hard-won reputation for excellence, the Hotel Splendide Royal entertains and immerses

guests in the vibrant, cultured spirit of its mother city.

Built as an aristocratic family home and later converted to house the headquarters of the Roman Maronite community, in 2001 the building was transformed into the 69-bedroom, baroque-style palace it is today. Inside, the décor mirrors its grand history and heritage, with the rooms themselves characterized by a sense of luxury and space that is uncannily reminiscent of boudoirs past; boiseries, fine draperies and antique furniture all contribute to the warm, seductive atmosphere.

With 52 Double Superior and Deluxe rooms and 17 suites – including the flagship Presidential Suite – Splendide Royal is seen as a symbol of the changes taking

Inviting guests to enjoy the timeless character of the Eternal City from its glorious terrace, this iconic hotel opens a window onto the lives of the 17th-century Roman aristocracy.

69 ROOMS AND SUITES   FITNESS CENTRE   GOURMET RESTAURANT   STUNNING VIEWS   WEDDINGS

VIA DI PORTA PINCIANA 14, 00187 ROME, ITALY
+39 06 421689 | RESERVATIONS@SPLENDIDEROYAL.COM | WWW.SPLENDIDEROYAL.COM

place within Rome's glittering hospitality sector. Blessed with a reputation for being full of the openness and familiarity usually reserved for close friends, it is known for a convivial atmosphere, comfortable surroundings and faultless service.

Showcasing decor and furniture familiar from ancient noble palaces – most notable of which is the huge Murano glass chandelier hanging above the main hall's geometric marble floors – the hotel's nod to the past is actually more of a considered bow. And with bespoke bedrooms offering a choice of balcony, walk-in closet or larger bathroom, rooms may be tailored to individual preferences. This, in many respects, is the ultimate definition of luxury.

Outside, the exclusive shops and designer boutiques of Rome's fashion industry are just a few minutes' walk away, in the legendary Piazza di Spagna and Via dei Condotti; nearby, the masterpieces of Canova and Caravaggio draw the lovers of art and sculpture to the Villa Borghese, its park adorned with multiple fountains

and statues, while the National Gallery of Modern Art, Piazza di Siena and the Globe theatre are also close at hand.

Indeed, it is this feeling of total immersion in Rome's history and heritage that makes Hotel Splendide Royal so popular with visitors from every background, culture and age group.

Introducing guests to its melting pot of classical decadence, tasteful luxury, modern amenities and 17th-century Roman overtones, the family-run hotel exhibits the typical Italian traits of style, panache and character. Such is the success of this formula that the Splendide Royal will soon be joined by a sister property in Paris.

With its striking interior, arresting views and the exquisite Mirabelle Restaurant on its doorstep, this remarkable hotel provides a door to the past, behind which lies a backdrop of contemporary luxury and impeccable style. When in Rome, there is no finer place to rest one's head. BHS

VILLA WALDKÖNIGIN

South Tyrol, Italy

Traditional art nouveau style meets contemporary comfort and luxury in this restored hilltop villa located almost 1.5 kilometres above sea level.

13 VILLA SUITES AND 14 MODERN PINE SUITES   BEAUTY LODGE   RESTAURANT
SAUNAS   SPA TREATMENTS   SWIMMING POOL

VILLA WALDKÖNIGIN, VIA DEL BOSCO 17, I-39027 SAN VALENTINO ALLA MUTA, SÜDTIROL – ALTO ADIGE, ITALY
+39 0473 634 559 | INFO@WALDKOENIGIN.COM | WWW.WALDKOENIGIN.COM

Completed in 1907, this Alpine masterpiece originally served as a holiday home for its creators before falling into disrepair and eventually undergoing a comprehensive restoration. Re-opening in 2010, the historic monument is now a leading destination hotel for relaxing, romantic breaks in the South Tyrol region of Italy.

Surrounded by mountains, meadows and fine gardens on the edge of the forest of San Valentino, Villa Waldkönigin commands sweeping views over the Muta Lake and up to the massif de l'Ortles.

Flanked by a modern south-west-facing extension, the painstakingly restored main building is enchanting in appearance and holds several of the guest rooms and suites. Meanwhile, housing the resort's swimming pool, Finnish sauna, steam bath, Kneipp area, solarium and Turkish bath, the pine-lined new wing features spacious suites and balconies overlooking King Ortles. As the area's highest mountain, it is well-known for winter sports including ski-touring, kite-surfing, hiking, mountain-biking and snowboarding. In summer the nearby Stelvio Pass is home to arguably the most exhilarating driving road in Europe, making the special Waldkönigin hire rate for a Jaguar F-Type cabriolet all the more appealing.

On the other hand, for those who prefer a more sedate speed of life, the hotel's indoor spa presents an astonishing array of massages, salt wraps, beauty therapies and body peels. There is a treatment to suit everyone, in fact, and the sensation afterwards of purified skin brushing up against warm sunshine and fresh mountain air is fairly hard to surpass. Emerging afterwards refreshed, if a touch somnolent, it is worth heading straight to the resort's restaurant for lunch or dinner. Attuned to diverse international tastes, the kitchen team prepare gourmet Tyrolean and Mediterranean specialities using the freshest ingredients gathered from local producers, growers and farmers. Unsurprisingly, breakfast here is pretty special, too.

With its Alpine meadows, extensive recreational pursuits and exceptional spa treatments, Villa Waldkönigin offers everything for a romantic wellness holiday in Val Venosta. Blending art and architecture, mountains and meadows, the old and the new, it provides an ancient escape with world-class facilities for modern-day relaxation and enjoyment. If stress or pressure is a popular poison these days, then Italy is the antidote and Villa Waldkönigin delivers just the right dosage. BHS

BORGO SANTO PIETRO

Tuscany, Italy

This glorious 13th-century hamlet has been restored and transformed by its Danish owners into a peerlessly attractive five-star luxury retreat on a 40-hectare estate.

Hidden away in a corner of the verdant Tuscan countryside, Borgo Santo Pietro has been lauded as one of the most alluring destinations in central Italy. The unique creative vision of fashion-turned-interior designer Jeanette and her property developer husband, Claus, it represents the ideal destination for couples, families and newlyweds seeking a different sort of escape.

Born from a personal dream to create the perfect family home, the dilapidated former village or *borgo* was purchased by the couple in 2001. Taking inspiration from their own observations and travels, the couple spent the next seven years meticulously pinpointing the details that would make the difference between creating a five-star hotel and the Borgo boutique experience. Opening in 2008, the ancient stone buildings had been transformed into a 16-room work of art that intertwines historic charm with modern luxury.

Welcomed by a cypress tree-lined driveway and over five hectares of landscaped gardens, it is impossible not to be struck by its beauty and sheer presence. Inside, the décor and detail of the principal social and reception areas continue the home-from-home theme: grand piano and giant farmhouse-table meet murals, oil paintings, winding stone staircases and worn leather armchairs opposite huge open fires. Downstairs, a weathered-brick wine cellar waits for guided explorations of its 850-plus boutique Italian and prestigious labels.

Similarly, the hotel's rooms and suites incorporate a warming blend of pastel colours, rich textiles and antique furniture. From the classical hand-painted frescoes on the walls of Sir Vincent and San Galgano, to the bare stone and undisturbed garden views of the Basilico and Maggiorana, they are all sublimely relaxing. Having said that, for the ultimate in regal privacy, space and

16 ROOMS AND SUITES   40-HECTARE ESTATE WITH 5-HECTARE GARDENS   BESPOKE CONCIERGE SERVICE

BOUTIQUE SPA   COOKING SCHOOL   FARM AND BIODYNAMIC CULINARY GARDENS   FRESHWATER INFINITY POOL

GRASS TENNIS COURTS   MICHELIN-STARRED RESTAURANT   RESIDENT ARTIST   TREEHOUSE BAR AND BRASSERIE

BORGO SANTO PIETRO, LOC. PALAZZETTO, 53012 CHIUSDINO (SIENA), ITALY
+39 0473 634 559 | RESERVATIONS@BORGOSANTOPIETRO.COM | WWW.BORGOSANTOPIETRO.COM

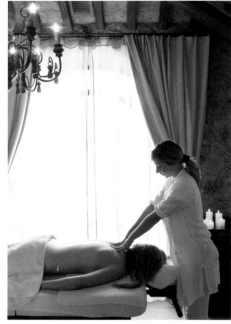

seclusion, nothing in the world comes close to the Santo Pietro Grand Suite. The cornerstone, both literally and figuratively, of Borgo, this 175-square-metre mini-apartment encapsulates and typifies the very essence of this special hotel. Standing alone at one end of the villa and replete with baroque furniture and artwork, it is the epitome of style, service and decadence. And in keeping with the meticulous attention to detail throughout, the bathrooms' free-standing bathtubs, twin pedestal sinks and separate Roman-style showers all compete for occupant attention.

If, however, by some divine miracle the inclination should ever arise to venture outside, a thorough investigation of the villa's public rooms and extensive grounds will be well-rewarded. Throw open the French doors onto the private balcony of the grand living-room and inhale the views of the Valle Serena's tumbling hills; wander freely among the surrounding olive groves, vineyards, forests and hilltop castles; or chat to executive chef Andrea Mattei and his team in their beloved vegetable and herb garden, a rural playground for this Michelin-Starred master.

In fact, when the time comes to refuel, Meo Modo serves what must surely be the most exquisite gourmet dishes available in central Italy, while the Treehouse Bar and Brasserie offers rustic Italian fare in a laid-back lounge ambience. With recipes and dishes designed in collaboration with Borgo's biodynamic culinary gardeners, healing herbs cultivated in the *orto* (kitchen garden), fresh artisan cheese made from Borgo sheep's milk and raw honey collected from the farm's own bees, this is a dedicated foodie destination with a pervasive ethos of self-sufficiency at its heart.

As a committed fan of the science and use of biodynamic vegetables – a fascination he shares with owners Claus and Jeanette Thottrup – Andrea is also at the helm of the Borgo Cooking School. Sharing a primal love of good food and the estate's farm-to-plate philosophy, the team of chefs and local cooks elucidate and educate with fun and good humour, instilling in their protégés a renewed sense of enthusiasm and experimentation.

Surrounded by organic farmland, vineyards, olive groves and vegetable gardens, the school offers a range of courses, classes and workshops for food lovers of all levels. In this saturated culture of celebrity chefs and endless TV bake-offs, the Borgo Cooking School represents a beacon of hope that our collective love of food will one day return to its simple origins. It really is that good.

Of course, a true countryside retreat would be incomplete without a spa. Along with its stunning freshwater infinity pool, the stone-built holistic centre showcases a combination of treatments, including deep-tissue massages by the fire and al fresco therapies in the canopied garden suite. It all adds up to an exceptionally attractive package, where attention to detail, friendly service and tailored experiences have become part everyday life.

And so, if a quiet, luxurious break is on the cards and Tuscany features prominently in the planning, let Borgo Santo Pietro seduce its way onto the shortlist. At only 30 minutes from Siena and an hour from Florence, this achingly beautiful hotel-estate is accessible enough to be easily reached and yet sufficiently secluded to hide away from the world outside. Simultaneously relaxing and captivating, educational and entertaining, it will transform the Tuscan holiday experience like a great Sangiovese transforms a rare steak. **BHS**

Opening in 2008, the ancient stone buildings had been transformed into a 16-room work of art that intertwines historic charm with modern luxury.

LOCANDA AL COLLE

Tuscany, Italy

Showcasing character, home-cooked cuisine and exemplary service, this converted 18th-century farmhouse employs a simple but effective idea to ensure guests feel at ease from the outset.

12 ROOMS AND SUITES   BAR   BUTLER SERVICE   OPEN APRIL-NOVEMBER   POOL   WEDDINGS

LOCANDA AL COLLE, VIA LA STRETTA 231, LOC. CAPEZZANO PIANORE, 55041 CAMAIORE, ITALY
+39 0584 915 195 | INFO@LOCANDAALCOLLE.IT | WWW.LOCANDAALCOLLE.COM

BOUTIQUE HOTEL SELECTION   178   EUROPE

Any perceived gulf between staff and guest is forgotten from the outset, and visitors are left with the impression they are simply arriving at a friend's country retreat rather than checking into a hotel.

It takes considerable vision to create a truly original offering in hospitality. With the ubiquitous big-name chains and many independent hotels seemingly blending into one homogeneous offering, operators are having to think of new approaches in order to differentiate their establishments from their competitors'. In beautiful Tuscany, where thousands of hotels and guesthouses jostle for business, the pressure to offer something new is forever present. Thankfully, Locanda al Colle's guests feel relaxed enough to enjoy themselves before they even enter their accommodation.

Having abandoned the traditional reception desk and replaced it with a friendly personal welcome, owner Riccardo meets visitors in the lobby and accompanies them to their rooms while their luggage is transported by Concierge. Consequently, any perceived gulf between staff and guest is forgotten from the outset, and visitors are left with the impression they are simply arriving at a friend's country retreat rather than checking into a hotel. In cultivating such an atmosphere of familial informality, the team have created a visitor experience like no other.

Located in the coastal province of Versilia, Locanda al Colle is decorated throughout with tasteful furnishings and unique items of classical art and local sculptures – another of the owner's signature touches. Spread over the three floors, the rooms are fitted with King-size Simmons beds, with most enjoying invigorating Hans-Grohe rain showers. The suites themselves benefit from private terraces with fireplaces, showcasing sweeping views of the Tuscan countryside. Outside, the heated saltwater swimming pool nestles in the grounds like a tempting, translucent pond.

Of course, this being Italy, the food constitutes a major part of the experience at Locanda al Colle. Cooking for guests three nights a week, chef Gian Luca recreates traditional dishes with contemporary flair using recipes lifted directly from his own cookbook. Twice a week guests may join in his open kitchen as he prepares dishes and, of course, he offers authentic cookery lessons for anyone looking to take home with them a slice or two of Locanda's gourmet inspiration.

For active types, there is naturally plenty to do in the surrounding area, from sailing in the Gulf of the Poets and trekking in the Apuan Alps, to cycling and rock-climbing in search of the legendary vistas of the verdant Tuscan countryside; nearby, the unspoiled beaches of Pietrasanta, Forte dei Marmi, and Viareggio yield impossibly pretty seascapes that constantly threaten to divert attention away from Locanda itself. That said, there is nothing more satisfying than returning after a day's exploration and opening the door to a hotel that feels like home.

Taken together with the stunning facilities, local attractions and indulgent food and wine, it all adds up to a friendly, infinitely personal experience. It can take a lot of effort and inspiration to mark an establishment out from the crowd these days but even little changes can make all the difference in the end. BHS

CA MARIA ADELE

Venice, Italy

Set inside a historic Venetian palazzo, this deeply decadent residence offers an engaging blend of history, culture and contemporary elegance in the world's most romantic city.

14 ROOMS   HONESTY BAR   IN-ROOM MASSAGES   KING-SIZE BEDS

MOROCCAN ROOF TERRACE   PRIVATE LANDING SPOT

CA MARIA ADELE, DORSODURO 111, 30123 VENICE, ITALY
+39 41 520 3078 | INFO@CAMARIAADELE.IT | WWW.CAMARIAADELE.IT

BOUTIQUE
HOTEL   180   EUROPE
SELECTION

La Sala Noire leaves visitors in no doubt that inhibitions should be abandoned at the door. Noire by name, noire by nature.

Aimed at travellers seeking culture and comfort without the crowds, Ca Maria Adele sits in a prestigious neighbourhood in the Dorsoduro art district, close to St Mark's Basilica. Heavy in Venetian and designed with a noticeable nod to an ancient era, the hotel is an object lesson in sympathetic restoration. Sitting opposite the imposing Santa Maria della Salute, near San Marco Square, its comprehensive transformation in 2004 has equipped guests with a window to the city's notoriously wealthy, seductive past.

Renovated by brothers Alessio and Nicola through their eponymous interior design brand, Campa&Campa, the interior is extravagantly decorated with indulgent damaschi fabrics, African wood furniture, marble fireplaces and Swarovski crystals.

Arriving either via land or water, guests are greeted in a Bohemian entrance hall dominated by a tatami floor, Moresque-style lamps and 19th-century black-marble fireplace. Dimly lit by period Murano chandeliers, the route through

the corridors to the artisanal bedrooms is soundproofed by heavily laden drapes, which adds to the illusion of a journey through Venice in a bygone age.

Each with its own distinctive style, the 14 bedrooms mix classical aromas, sounds, moods and even dress codes to recreate the atmosphere of epochs past. Spread over four floors, five of the rooms deserve special mention; exotically themed, these individually designed concept suites employ indulgent fabrics, evocative scents and impeccable décor to escort occupants back into 16th-century Venice.

With the fragrance of Bulgarian rose and a rich blood-red brocade adorning the walls, the Doge's Room invites guests to unwind in old-style opulence, while the Fireplace Room – dominated by an imposing engraved marble chimney – employs a scented interior to stimulate deep thought and contemplation.

Elsewhere, heavily influenced by the culture and architecture of North-West Africa, the Moorish Room invites its occupants to surrender their hectic,

tech-laden lives, and the Oriental Room demands nothing more than a commitment to quiet reflection and meditation. Inspired by the charm and romance of the ancient silk route and draped with antique gold, it opens an esoteric door to Venice's colourful past.

Finally, radiating mystique and intrigue, the Black-Orchid-scented La Sala Noire exhibits a dark, hedonistic side, leaving visitors in no doubt that inhibitions should be abandoned at the door. Noire by name, noire by nature.

Unsurprisingly, breakfast here is more of an event than a routine. Served either in-room or in the grand lounge, the lavish menu is occasionally extended onto the Moroccan-inspired terrace which also doubles as the spot for pre-dinner aperitifs and evening nightcaps.

With a merciful lack of child-friendly facilities and space, Ca Maria Adele provides the perfect retreat for couples seeking a romantic break. In fact, if family-planning considerations are on the agenda in the immediate future, it is well worth a visit beforehand. BHS

BYBLOS ART HOTEL

Verona, Italy

Located just 15 minutes from Verona and bursting with Italian style and character,
this glorious 16th-century villa unashamedly celebrates the right to be different.

Merging 59 luxurious bedrooms with an assortment of delightful eccentricities, Byblos is probably the largest – and certainly the most fun – hotel in the viticultural province of Valpolicella. Filled with a lively concoction of paintings, sculptures and frescoes, the interior of the Veronese Renaissance building is a heady mix of classical influences and contemporary design; ornate chandeliers and antique tables sit alongside office-style furniture pods and over 180 items of colourful, frequently whimsical, modern art.

Each completely different, the rooms themselves are plush and limitlessly imaginative. The hotel's designer, Alessandro Mendini, has contrasted old and new to quite startling effect and a stroll through the corridors and spa reveals the extent of his vision. Simultaneously striking and illogical, the designs and displays are always playful. Unexpected objects are everywhere: a businessman fashioned from bubble gum hangs from the lobby balcony in a despairing free-fall; gleaming statues of Kate Moss guard the entrance; Anish Kapoor's metal-works bend light in unpredictable directions; and Damian Hirst's iconic memento mori provide subtle-but-persistent reminders not to take leisure – or life – for granted.

Fortunately, the quirks continue throughout the accommodation. All different – and, of course, colourful – the bedrooms feature unique, slightly crazy interpretations of regular features and furnishings: minibars secreted in brightly painted cupboards; modern mirrors

---

Byblos's bedrooms feature unique, slightly crazy interpretations of regular features and furnishings.

---

bearing faint resemblance to their classic, gilt-framed relatives; dizzying mosaics and plastic lamps adorning walls and bedside tables. From the Deluxe and Superior rooms to the larger Junior suites and up, it's all about amusement.

Perhaps inevitably, the twin bathrooms of the flagship Presidential Suite take things a little more seriously. Decadent marble meets bathtub and shower – simple – and the underlying message has clearly been recognized and respected by the designers: it is all very well to laugh and have fun with the guests during the day, at dinner and over drinks but don't, whatever the motivation, mess with the morning ritual.

Meanwhile, a walk in the extensive gardens reveals an intricate network of secluded lawns and alcoves which eventually lead to a vast outdoor swimming pool at the rear of the villa. Located in a

59 ROOMS · BAR · FITNESS CENTRE · POOL · RESTAURANT · SAUNA · SPA

BYBLOS ART HOTEL, VIA CEDRARE 78, 37029 CORRUBBIO DI NEGARINE, SAN PIETRO IN CARIANO (VERONA), ITALY
+39 045 685 5555 | RESERVATION@BYBLOSARTHOTEL.COM | WWW.BYBLOSARTHOTEL.COM

BOUTIQUE HOTEL SELECTION · 182 · EUROPE

quiet, sun-soaked position under the gaze of Verona marble fountains, it is surrounded by trees and plants, with chaises-longues dotted around the edge.

Nearby, along a little-known pathway above the main pool area, lies a secret, adult-only chill-out area with Jacuzzis, daybeds and all-day complimentary fruit.

Elsewhere, Espace Byblos – the hotel's indoor spa – provides a somewhat more sincere but no less entertaining escape from the real world. Massages are a speciality, and regenerative beauty therapies – using amber and real gold – are typical of the extravagant and thoroughly exclusive nature of the Pompeii-themed facility. With sauna, hot tub, steam room and lengthy list of treatments, the spa presents a blissful escape from almost-inevitable sensory overload.

Between them, Byblos's two restaurants manage to cover the entire taste spectrum of Valpolicella, accompanied by over 300 carefully selected labels from the hotel's 15th-century cellar. As the newly launched flagship eatery, Amistà 33 is dedicated to the art of fine Italian cuisine. Inspired by a similar level of creativity that underpins the hotel's own raison d'être, Executive chef Marco Perez creates modern interpretations of classical Italian flavours, and his six-to-nine-course tasting menu is definitely worthy of closer inspection.

On the other hand, Atelier Restaurant's re-interpretations of regional and international dishes make the best of the organically cultivated fruit and vegetables from the hotel's private garden. Between them it adds up to a thoroughly satisfying gastronomic experience that

enhances, rather than detracts from, the wonderfully unconventional atmosphere throughout the hotel. Indeed, if the Byblos philosophy is abstract and alternative, the food itself is deliciously familiar.

Conceived like a permanent exhibition in a museum of modern art, the philosophy here is underpinned by a pervasive, unmistakable sense of fun. Juxtaposing the distinctive and tasteful with the weird and frequently wonderful examples of sculptures, paintings and abstract modern art, the furnishings are as much a part of the Byblos experience as is the luxury and service.

Whatever the holiday duration it is always a curiosity to behold, but in an anodyne world of bland uniformity and computer-aided design, it is nonetheless always a welcome one. BHS

HOTEL SEBASTIAN'S

Amsterdam, Netherlands

Replete with colourful, dramatic décor this ultra-chic townhouse hotel is the perfect location from which to take advantage of the city's vibrant anything-goes atmosphere.

33 ROOMS   BAR   BIKE HIRE   BREAKFAST   CENTRAL LOCATION   FAMILY ROOMS

HOTEL SEBASTIAN'S, KEIZERSGRACHT 15, 1015 CC, AMSTERDAM, NETHERLANDS
+31 20 423 23 42 | INFO@HOTELSEBASTIANS.NL | WWW.HOTELSEBASTIANS.NL

BOUTIQUE HOTEL SELECTION   186   EUROPE

Situated right next to one of Amsterdam's most picturesque canals in the heart of the city, Sebastian's is a contemporary boutique establishment with an innovative design and distinctly sophisticated character. Created by owners Eric and Petra Toren and based around the same service-orientated philosophy as its nearby sister property, The Toren, this modish, cosy, welcoming retreat is nevertheless a distinctive proposition in its own right. The location alone is a key appeal; just a stone's throw from the Jordaan district's numerous cafés and restaurants, and Haarlemmerstraat's shops and outdoor markets, Sebastian's is comfortably one of best-positioned hotels in Amsterdam.

Inside, the news is just as encouraging; combining warm, sultry colours with refined furnishings and décor, the recently renovated interior is the inspired creation of renowned Dutch designer Wim van de Oudeweetering. His unorthodox-but-ingenious approach also helped achieve The Toren's unique look and layout. Imbuing Sebastian's with a refreshingly unconventional air – an underlying signature theme of his work – Wim's design style is halfway between plush and minimalist. The bathrooms are immaculate yet classically appealing, and the corridors are adorned with wall-mounted vases containing blooming tree branches. It all suggests a novel, quirky approach to interior design and presents a thoroughly welcome change to the standardized offering of the ubiquitous big-name chains.

The rooms at Sebastian's, several of which feature a soaking tub, patio or courtyard and either canal or garden views, vary from short-stay-size to full-on family affairs. Ideal for guests seeking a compact, clutter-free base in a central location, the Small Rooms fit the bill for those who travel light; there are self-explanatory medium-size options but it is the Large Rooms that prove most attractive to families. Stretching up to 55 square metres in size, these generously proportioned spaces may be specified with additional beds and are suitable for guests seeking a more spacious environment during their stay.

Although there is no restaurant within the hotel, Sebastian's nevertheless serves a variety of moreish snacks and lunchtime dishes in the effortlessly trendy bar. Enjoyed with a glass of wine or cold beer, these delicious appetizers provide welcome refreshment after a day's shopping and exploration, or hunger-pang pacifiers prior to dinner in one of the many restaurants at the heart of this beautiful city. In the morning, a buffet-style breakfast sets the tone before the next adventures begin. Naturally, bike rentals are easily organized and theatre performances, concerts and restaurants may all be reserved through the hotel; indeed, the genial, expertly briefed staff are never less than delighted to help with enquiries of any nature and complexity, a fact that goes some way to explaining Sebastian's formidable fourth-place position for service among all hotels in the Netherlands. Having experienced varying levels of incivility and indifference from hotel staff throughout the world – many of whom fail to grasp the concept of a smile being completely cost-free – it is wonderfully refreshing to meet such friendly, helpful staff. As with The Toren, employees at Sebastian's clearly enjoy their work and they genuinely love meeting guests. This is a relatively rare quality in hotels these days, yet it is evident in both establishments from arrival to departure and every moment in between. BHS

THE TOREN

Amsterdam, Netherlands

*Substitute the risqué and rude for romance and decadence
in one of the city's most distinctive and charming hotels.*

Situated just 15 minutes' walk from Centraal Station, this restored 17th-century former canal building provides a merciful refuge in the midst of Amsterdam's tourist mayhem. Inviting guests to sidestep the city's more salacious attractions, the historic townhouse is surrounded by ancient cobbled streets and historic stonework bridges. Inside, the burlesque décor is tinged with shades of neoclassicism, with plenty of deep rich golds and purples, antique mirrors and smoked glass. Each of the 38 individually styled rooms is influenced by heavy theatrical overtones, complete with ornate chandeliers and lush fabrics. Bespoke touches include a choice of ensuite steam room or bedside hot tub, either of which make it disconcertingly easy to forget life back home.

Meanwhile, with an extensive list of wines, champagnes and cocktails, The Toren's intricate main bar opens a window onto the city's artistic and mercantile past. Featuring antique lighting and a giant mural reputedly painted by Rembrandt's own studio assistant, the room is dominated by a floor-to-ceiling mahogany drinks cabinet. Fortunately, this also provides the backdrop to breakfast, where genial, beautifully trained staff assist with the freshly prepared buffet.

For those wishing to venture further afield in search of sustenance, there are dozens of restaurants and bistros situated within strolling distance of the hotel, as are many of Amsterdam's more prolific tourist attractions. From guided shopping trips, canal cruises and cultural excursions, to historical tours and eye-opening adventures in the red-light district, it's all there.

The best part about staying at The Toren, however, tends to come at the end of a day's sightseeing, when the hotel's warm-hearted atmosphere inveigles the mind back to normality. Relaxing in the bar with a cheese platter or club sandwich, it is entirely possible to turn both a deaf ear and a blind eye to the stag weekends and suggestive distractions corrupting the world outside. After all, this particular city was once famed primarily for its beauty, history and rich cultural diversity, and there is no reason why it shouldn't be these days, too. **BHS**

> Featuring a giant mural reputedly painted by Rembrandt's own studio assistant, The Toren's main bar provides the backdrop to breakfast and is dominated by a floor-to-ceiling mahogany drinks cabinet.

38 ROOMS | BAR | ENSUITE HOT TUBS OR STEAM ROOMS

THE TOREN, KEIZERSGRACHT 164, 1015 CZ AMSTERDAM, NETHERLANDS
+31 020 622 63 52 | RESERVATIONS@THETOREN.NL | WWW.THETOREN.NL

HERANGTUNET

Heggenes, Norway

Framed by woods, lakes and glaciers, this converted farm building invites guests to live the authentic Nordic farmhouse experience in a wild, gloriously unpredictable outdoor world.

5 ROOMS AND 4 SUITES APPLE TV DINING AREA ESPRESSO MACHINE KITCHENETTE

HERANGTUNET, VØLBUSVEGEN 17, 2940 HEGGENES, NORWAY
+47 613 416 65 | INFO@HERANGTUNET.COM | WWW.HERANGTUNET.COM

BOUTIQUE
HOTEL   192   EUROPE
SELECTION

With a lengthy list of outdoor activities including fjording, hunting, boating, skiing, fishing, riding and walking, the big test for guests will be learning when – or how – to say no.

A member of De Historiske, a unique collection of Norway's finest hotels and restaurants, Herangtunet is perched 500 metres above sea level in the southern central Valdres province. Part of a self-contained mini-complex of traditional wooden outhouses, the building was converted a decade ago by its Dutch visionaries, Marco and Marie-José Robeerst.

Literally translated the restored 'farm-garden' sits deep within a forest, and forms a welcome outpost in a feral, untamed landscape. With a lengthy list of outdoor activities nearby, including fjording, hunting, boating, skiing, fishing, riding and walking, the big test for guests will be learning when – or how – to say no.

In addition to the five standard rooms, four themed suites are also available. Named after the hosts' favourite worldwide destinations, each captures the character of the ancient farm steading and each carries its own unique story. As a rustic mix of wood, slate, fur and fire, the Aspen Royal boasts deep leather armchairs, a king-size double bed and a traditional-style bathroom with wooden bath and separate shower. Close by, the London suite was designed to mirror a City gentlemen's club; velvet, leather, marble and granite meet crackling fire and crocodile-skin wallpaper to create a sophisticated escape from the outside world.

Meanwhile, as a clear contradiction between the dynamics of the City That Never Sleeps and the isolation of Herangtunet, the New York City is a suite of stark contrasts. From the effortless chic of the Willy Guhl loop chairs to the warmth of the French army stove, its simplicity proves as cosseting as it is striking. Alternatively, as Herangtunet's largest suite, the Rome Imperial presents a golden opportunity to elope to the ancient empire. Exhibiting typical dramatic ambience – the frescoed ceiling inspired by the Baths of Caracalla, for example, or the whirlpool bath surrounded by Bisazza mosaics – this is where decadence meets extravagance. Even the distinctive Illy coffee machine offers a classic touch of Italian craftsmanship.

Perhaps inevitably, the food at Herangtunet is high up on everyone's priority list and the Norwegian-influenced French cuisine works beautifully. Come refuelling time, the chefs' colourful grazing platters and local specialities are best consumed outside, and should any of the local fishing spots yield positive results these too may be barbecued al fresco.

Therein lies the magic of this outstanding farmhouse hideout; although its founders drew on multinational influences when they conceived the idea, it remains an unmistakably Scandinavian experience. From dipping into crystal clear lakes, hiking in the Jotunheimen National Park and skiing or dog-sledding on the slopes of nearby Beitostolen, this utterly captivating environment could only ever be a native Norwegian adventure. BHS

VILA JOYA
HOME, RESTAURANT AND SPA
Albufeira, Portugal

Set on a hill in the pretty former fishing village, this Oriental palazzo and Two-Michelin-Starred restaurant offer quietude, decadence and fine dining on Portugal's Atlantic coast.

Almost 40 years ago, Dr Klaus Jung and his wife Claudia travelled to the Algarve in search of a family home. Selecting an area of land, they discovered an unfinished house that possessed neither electricity nor running water but which captured their imagination nonetheless. Over the next few years, the couple transformed the property into a summer home and eventually opened it as Vila Joya, in 1982. Nowadays it is run by her daughter, Joy, who has with the help of her team – most notably long-serving executive chef Dieter Koschina – maintained it as one of the country's leading boutique hotels.

12 ROOMS AND 8 SUITES   GARDEN   HOT TUB   GOLF PACKAGES   GYM   OCEAN VIEWS   SAUNA   SPA
TWO-MICHELIN-STARRED RESTAURANT   TWO SWIMMING POOLS

VILA JOYA, ESTRADA DA GALÉ , 8200-416 ALBUFEIRA, ALGARVE, PORTUGAL
+35 1 289 591 795 | INFO@VILAJOYA.COM | WWW.VILAJOYA.COM

BOUTIQUE
HOTEL   194   EUROPE
SELECTION

Led by Portugal's first and only Two-Michelin-Starred chef, Vila Joya's kitchen team generates brand-new recipes on a nightly basis.

With a total of 12 rooms and eight unique suites, all but one with boundless ocean views and either a balcony or terrace, Vila Joya has carved out its own little niche in Portuguese hospitality. From the Junior Suite with its indigenous cork flooring, freestanding bath and private garden, to the penthouse-style Royal Suite Joia and everything in between, there is a level of luxury to suit all tastes. The rooms, on the other hand, present a somewhat more modest proposition but with the usual Vila Joya detail, quirks, extras and refinements; indeed, a couple may be even twinned with adjoining suites to make them family-friendly.

Unsurprisingly, given the calibre of the hotel and its location, abundant sea views come as standard and air conditioning features throughout.

Meanwhile, every other feature and facility – the 12,000-bottle wine cellar, the verdant gardens, the golf academy, the exotic massages and detoxifying body scrubs of the in-house spa – help attract a loyal following of repeat customers. But, however irresistible these amenities may be, they are but contributory elements in

JOY JUNG

A director of Vila Joya for 12 years prior to taking over from her parents in 2013, Munich native Joy is conscious of the need to continue the legacy of her interior designer mother, Claudia. Created and cultivated during her tenure, the villa's very style, hospitality and essence are still noticeable today, some 20 years after Claudia passed away. Studiously referring to Vila Joya as a home, rather than a hotel, Joy has worked hard to emulate her mother's achievements and credits the success of the business to the friendliness of the team, the villa's perfect location and its apparent ability to reach out and touch the souls of guests and set their spirits free.

DIETER KOSCHINA

One of Portugal's most respected and decorated chefs, Austrian Dieter secured his first Michelin Star at Vila Joya in 1995, and his second four years later. Creating a new six-course menu with head chef Stefan Langmann each evening – an exceptional undertaking for a restaurant of this calibre – he achieved his most notable success in 2012 when he entered, at No. 45, the list of the World's 50 Best Restaurants. By the following year Dieter's establishment had climbed eight places before peaking at number 22, in 2014. Using his unique inspiration, creativity and dedication to create the perfect dish, he is proud of the flexibility and autonomy afforded by owner Joy. The fact he has retained his twin Michelin Stars for 16 years, despite the daily changing menu, highlights just how much skill and talent this gentleman really has.

the greater Vila Joya experience. The final ingredient, as it were, that has all but exclusively ensured the longevity and success of this unique establishment over the last 25 years, is its restaurant. Led by Dieter, Portugal's first and only Two-Michelin-Starred chef, the kitchen brigade produces the country's finest dishes and manages to generate brand-new ideas and recipes on a nightly basis. Such is the level of skill, commitment and imagination required to turn out six different tasting menus each week, it is nigh impossible to think of anyone else ever filling his shoes. Because, when all is said and done, there is nothing more compelling than a holiday venue that has become a recognized dining destination in its own right. This is precisely the achievement of the team at Vila Joya, and there could be no greater compliment to Claudia, its founder and original creative force. **BHS**

Surrounded by the rolling hillsides, terracotta roofs and twisted vines of the rural villages so typical of northern Portugal, Carmo's has carved out a very particular niche for itself. Completed in 2012, the hotel was sympathetically constructed on the site of an ancient farmhouse and draws heavily on northern Portuguese culture. Full of attendant personality, the three luxury suites and 12 Prestige Rooms present the archetypal boutique experience; subtle décor, immaculately detailed furnishings and opulent bathrooms are mandatory. Downstairs, the walls are adorned with old-school sepia photos and the bookshelves creak with both classical and contemporary titles. Deep in the basement, the private Divine spa offers aromatherapy massages and unique rituals such as the Goats' Milk Bath. Meanwhile, filled floor-to-ceiling, the bar will occupy connoisseurs for the duration of their holiday.

Of course, such hedonism could always be ignored in favour of a day's relaxation by the outdoor pool. With panoramic views and a glass of champagne or local Sangria, there's little inclination to seek entertainment elsewhere. Nevertheless, do try to remain strong, for there is much to be discovered on the doorstep, the myriad distractions within touching distance of the hotel include guided tours, drawing classes, riding, hiking and rustic picnics.

And when the time comes to recharge, Carmo's offers some of the most flavoursome cuisine this side of the Atlantic. Employing a wide range of ingredients, many of which are grown in the hotel kitchen garden, the chefs draw on an extensive variety of the most traditional Portuguese tastes. The wine list, naturally, is proudly and exclusively Portuguese, and fortunate visitors this season could be among the first to sample the hotel's own label. Produced in-house at the hotel Wine Atelier from local grapes, it will soon become the unsung hero of the sommelier's cellar. Indeed, if a trip to Portugal is in the diary this year, a break at Carmo's comes highly recommended. Best to book it up swiftly, however, before the first vintage runs out. BHS

Full of attendant personality, the three luxury suites and 12 Prestige Rooms present the archetypal boutique experience; subtle décor, immaculately detailed furnishings and opulent bathrooms are mandatory.

PALÁCIO BELMONTE

Lisbon, Portugal

Once the residence of a noble Portuguese family, this lavishly restored former stately home was recently branded one of the coolest hotels in the world.

10 SUITES   7 TERRACES   AIRPORT TRANSFER   ART   BOOKS   BUTLER SERVICE   INFINITY POOL   PIANO

PALÁCIO BELMONTE, PÁTIO DE DOM FRADIQUE 14, 1100-624 LISBON, PORTUGAL
+351 21 881 6600 | RESERVATIONS@PALACIOBELMONTE.COM | WWW.PALACIOBELMONTE.COM

BOUTIQUE
HOTEL
SELECTION   200   EUROPE

In this saturated world of bland brands, it takes vision, imagination and a profoundly grand design to create something truly special and distinctive. The grandest of them all is Palácio Belmonte.

When Frenchman Frédéric Coustols and his wife Maria purchased Palácio Belmonte in 1994, they set about restoring and transforming the 15th-century building into a regal retreat. Reopening six years later, after a painstaking rebuild, this agonizingly beautiful hotel has since become the most exclusive best-kept secret in Lisbon.

Accessed through a large red door in a quiet courtyard only metres from the tourist crowds in the heart of Lisbon, Belmonte's 3,700 square metres are spread over several floors. With eleven suites and a thoroughly welcome dearth of such conventional amenities as televisions and reception desks, the palace has seemingly created an entirely new class of its own. Prioritizing authenticity over gimmickry, and light, space and landscapes over ostentation, it represents a glorious departure from the cynical predictability of franchised establishments.

Helped by innovative touches including a natural ventilation system and the deliberate positioning of a series of mini-staircases in place of elevators, the design favours extensive use of traditional materials and decorative touches. Of these, the most striking are the 3,800 blue-and-white Portuguese tiles dating from the 18th century. Mounted on 59 panels in sitting-rooms, libraries and suites throughout the hotel, they are arguably one of the building's most congenial and conspicuous distinguishing features. The magnificent Maria Ursula ballroom accommodates 17 of these panels alone, in addition to three enormous chandeliers hanging high from a painted marble ceiling. And yet despite its beauty and grandeur, the 100-square-metre room is studiously, gloriously subtle and unassuming.

For those in search of rest and reflection, meanwhile, both the Belmonte Cultural Café and the Governor's Room provide the requisite atmosphere in which to read and relax in the presence of music, contemporary art and history. Similarly, the 11 suites themselves represent the very essence of life at Palácio Belmonte. From the enormous Gil Vicente with its terrace and winter garden, to the Padre Himalaya – a romantic double arranged over two levels and boasting 360-degree views – each one offers a combination of eye-widening vistas and fastidious attention to detail. Perhaps more than anything, this tenacious insistence on perfection is a reflection of the hosts' commitment to accomplishing their dream. To recreate this exceptional boutique hotel, Frédéric and Maria first had to generate and then promote an entirely new attitude, outlook and lifestyle. There are, of course, other perfectly restored establishments from which to choose throughout Europe, but none of them so finely combine the seductions of history, art, culture, luxury, space and peace. In this saturated world of character-free franchises and bland brands, it takes vision, imagination and a profoundly grand design to create something truly special and distinctive. Without doubt, the grandest of them all is Palácio Belmonte, considered by many to be the most beautiful hotel in the world. BHS

AMBASSADOR À L'OPÉRA

Zürich, Switzerland

A perennially popular choice for discerning visitors seeking cultural enlightenment, a refreshing city break and a spot of retail therapy, the Ambassador à l'Opéra has long been the model for others to follow. Part of the former Uto Castle dating from 1898, the neo-baroque-style hotel attracts tourists, holidaymakers and business people from all over the world. Situated just steps away from innumerable galleries, museums and the great eponymous lake, the hotel's fortuitous position is ideal for sightseeing and exploring. From its location opposite the great Zürich Opera House, roaming excursions end up more like enjoyable jaunts rather than treks.

From its unique location close to Zürich's abundant cultural attractions – most notably the famous Opera House – this glorious boutique hotel provides the ideal base for exploring the city.

45 ROOMS | BAR | CENTRALLY LOCATED | ELECTRONICALLY ADJUSTABLE BEDS | RESTAURANT | ROOF TERRACE

AMBASSADOR À L'OPÉRA, FALKENSTRASSE 6, 8008 ZÜRICH, SWITZERLAND
+41 44 258 98 98 | WELCOME@AMBASSADORHOTEL.CH | WWW.AMBASSADORHOTEL.CH

BOUTIQUE HOTEL SELECTION | 202 | EUROPE

Boasting one of the highest quality lifestyles in the world, Zürich also enjoys a culinary scene to rival the globe's gastronomic must-go cities. It should therefore come as no surprise that the cuisine at Ambassador à l'Opéra is of a similar calibre. Prioritizing sustainable fish, executive chef Pierre Meyer and his team source fresh, predominantly local ingredients to prepare world-class dishes in Restaurant Opera. And with 'Enjoyment 10', his monthly tasting menu, returning guests may sample the very best fare knowing that their particular selections will likely be one-offs. Surrounded by Surrealist-baroque wall paintings and facing out over arresting boulevard views below, it makes for a deliciously satisfying recipe of an evening, in more ways than one. With special pre-opera dining packages available, including a glass of champagne, three-course meal, two show tickets and a souvenir programme signed by the theatre's director, Andreas Homoki, the Ambassador's Zürich Opera experience is one of the most entertaining and exclusive anywhere in the world.

During a stay here, occasions will inevitably arise when even the allure of the Zürich's infinite cultural distractions and Bahnhofstrasse's seductive boutiques will fail to tempt visitors out to play. Fortunately, the hotel provides a generous array of diversions, including an engaging bar-restaurant, weekly wine-tasting on the rooftop terrace and dreamy al fresco picnics by the lake. And when the day's activities come to an end and tiredness takes over, there are some imaginative touches here that aren't typically found in establishments of any size around the world: pillow menus, for example, allow guests to select their preferred shape, material and resistance; and if long morning lie-ins are a priority and breakfast is missed accordingly it may be taken in another establishment altogether, courtesy of a clever agreement with the hotel across the road. It is little quirks like this that showcase the care behind the Ambassador à l'Opéra experience.

On the face of it, there cannot be many hotels that are situated so close to a world-famous venue such as the Zürich Opera with all its attendant attractions. But so diverse is the culture, art, history and architectural beauty here that Zürich both demands and deserves a hotel that places guests at the centre of the action. Mercifully, this delightfully relaxed establishment fulfils that role with a reassuring confidence. **BHS**

11 MIRRORS

Kyiv, Ukraine

*A resolutely independent establishment in the heart of Ukraine's capital,
this hotel, part of the Design Hotels community, combines
heavyweight heritage, exceptional facilities and a very personal touch.*

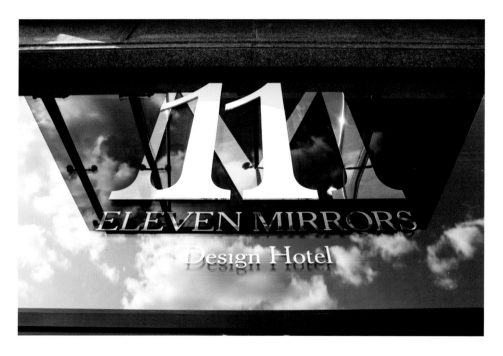

Located just a few metres from the National Opera House and offering a big-hearted Ukrainian hug of a welcome to this fascinating historic city, 11 Mirrors has been both shaped and inspired by world-renowned Heavyweight Champion, Wladimir Klitschko.

Named after the 'essential qualities of the accomplished personality' – Curiosity; Optimism; Courage; Passion; Creativity; Sense of humour; Independence; Confidence; Reliability; Generosity and finally Harmony – the hotel blends stylish accommodation with environmentally friendly technology to create a one-off visitor experience. Each of the 49 air-conditioned guestrooms and suites incorporates contemporary interior design with the latest technology for the ultimate hospitality experience. All rooms feature rainfall showers, while certain

49 ROOMS AND SUITES   CENTRAL LOCATION   LOUNGE BAR   RESTAURANT

11 MIRRORS, 34A BOHDANA KHMELYTKOGO STREET, KYIV, UKRAINE
+380 44 581 1111 | INFO@11MIRRORS-HOTEL.COM | WWW.11MIRRORS-HOTEL.COM

Each of the air-conditioned guestrooms and suites incorporates contemporary interior design with the latest technology.

upgrades add open bars, city views and walk-in showers.

Located on the mezzanine level, the informal restaurant offers Continental-style breakfasts, light lunches and refined dinner menus that bring together a collection of local, national and international dishes. Meanwhile, situated within two minutes' walk of the hotel, the Leonardo Wellness Club shares an exclusive arrangement with 11 Mirrors; guests are provided with special rates and offers for its exhaustive repertoire of treatments, remedies and therapies.

Returning to the hotel after an afternoon of massages and relaxation, Kyiv's historical quarter tends to prove something of a distraction. From the ancient Golden Gates to the famous St Sophia Cathedral and charming collection of 19th-century buildings, the city carries with it a certain mystique that begs to be further explored. Coincidentally, this allure extends to most other aspects and areas of the Ukrainian capital. Bisected by the Dnipro River and known for its religious architecture, secular monuments and history museums, the city has prospered during the last years, yet the majority of its history and heritage remains untouched. With so much to see and experience, Kyiv is a shamefully underrated holiday and short-break destination that is just waiting to be discovered. It is a window onto an unexplored world, updated and uprated for the 21st century through the reflection of 11 Mirrors. BHS

DIRECTORY